DON'T YOU

T0090068

DON'T YOU EVER

My Mother and
Her Secret Son

MARY CARTER
BISHOP

HARPER

NEW YORK • LONDON • TORONTO • SYDNEY

HARPER

FIRST HARPER PAPERBACKS EDITION PUBLISHED 2019.

Designed by Fritz Metsch

Library of Congress Cataloging-in-Publication Data has been applied for.

ISBN 978-0-06-240074-1 (pbk.)

19 20 21 22 23 LSC 10 9 8 7 6 5 4 3 2 1

For Mom and Ronnie
Side by side on these pages

CONTENTS

DON'T YOU EVER

PART I

TWO

FUNERALS

Losing the Brother I Hardly Knew

Ronnie's foster mother, Polly Hall, took many
pictures of a joyful Ronnie at her family's farm
near Blacksburg, Virginia.

I sit alone by Ronnie's body at the funeral home in Vinton,
Virginia, on February 20, 1991.

They found him the day before, sitting up in bed, clip-on
reading lamp shining above his head. He was fully clothed:
khaki pants, a short-sleeved button-down shirt, a down vest,
Hush Puppies, and brown socks. The uniform he wore to his
barbershop on Vinton's main street. The illness that had tor-
mented Ronnie finally soaked his mattress with blood and
stopped his heart.

I reach over and place my right hand over his. Though cold
and rubbery, it feels familiar. I loved to watch those long, wide

fingers gently tap the heads of little boys, angling them just so for his scissors. Those giant hands were careful.

I always wanted a brother or a sister. I'd watch kids running wild across the fields on farms near my childhood home, two hours from Vinton. It looked like pure elation to me, a gang of children squealing in unison as their quick legs tore through the alfalfa.

At our tenant house, I played alone. Surrounded by pastures, the old farmhouse was the last structure along the winding road of a rich man's estate. Children lived a hike away across vast fields. Most of them weren't a natural fit for me. They were rich. Or they were too old. Or they were too young. Or my mama didn't know their mama.

There was, though, for a while, a boy. They said he was my cousin. Tall, thin, ten years older, he was a mystery to me. He disappeared when I was seven. I was thirty-two before I learned by accident from a government document that he was not my cousin; he was my half brother. When I confronted my mother, she thought I already knew. I was a prize-winning journalist, a professional observer of the human condition, but I had missed the most significant fact of my life, a secret hiding in plain sight.

I PULL MY reporter's pad from my pocketbook. Tomorrow the undertakers will close the lid on Ronnie's casket, and I will never see him again.

He'd probably curse me for putting him on display like this, I think. I can hear him now: *Goddammit, woman, leave me alone!* But I want his friends to come think about him and say goodbye. For them, and for me, and even for my brother.

Ronnie made his living holding people's heads in his hands. The rest of the time, he kept to himself. He hated being stared at, but he loved it when people had their backs to him in his barber chair. Then they could hear him, but they couldn't see him. As he snipped away, I'd watch from a chair in his waiting area.

In him, I saw my long, skinny arms and legs. We shared a reverence for old forests, a certain Southern cadence of speech, and a quick, explosive laugh. In his voice I heard a low gurgle like our granddaddy's, and in the way he saw the world, our mother's many fears.

In Ronnie's last years, he fed me piece by little piece what had happened to him as a child. Each revelation was a punch to my heart. I'd had it so good. He'd had the exact opposite.

I process hard times by writing them down, a habit from my days as a newspaper reporter. My long neck tilts permanently to the right from four decades of hauling a heavy bag of notebooks, recorder, and camera from my right shoulder. That bag came with me on many visits with Ronnie, but he never let me photograph him or record him. Except for two minutes and seventeen seconds on a cassette tape—a recording he stopped when he grew self-conscious—I have no record of him as he was at the end. All I can do is commit him to memory with my words.

He was a tall, odd-looking skeleton of a man who commanded his barbershop with a flap of his bony arms and a low voice that sounded as if it came from deep within a hollow tube.

His customers roared at his tales, loaded with "hells," "damns," and "sons-a-bitches." He told them stories about rascally old hermits up in the mountains and the bears, snakes,

and wild turkeys he'd tracked deep within the central Appalachians. He had left school in the eighth grade and educated himself later reading history books at the public library.

On my first visit to his barbershop, I thought Ronnie was somebody else. He'd been a young man the last time I saw him. Now it was 1987. He had changed. His forehead jutted out like the prow of a ship. His nose was bigger. His eyes sank deeper within his facial bones. His lips, once on the thin side, had blown up. *(How did the undertaker manage to stuff his oversized tongue into his mouth?)*

His straight, coarse silver hair stood out stiffly from his scalp, a dense forest of steel wires. My hair was thin and fine like my daddy's. Ronnie, though, had our mother's hair, thick as a wig. Even she couldn't deny the resemblance.

Ronnie stood with his right foot resting on his left, like a six-foot-three stork. His huge hands splayed out from his thin wrists and violently whapped the hydraulic lift of the barber chair to lock a customer into place. Sometimes the men looked a little frightened.

Ronnie's face flew into crazy mechanics when something amused him. Not much did; or rather, it had to be novel or really clever or blasphemous. As soon as he heard the thing, he'd abruptly lift his mighty head a couple of inches as if electrically jolted. Then, just as quickly, he'd drop it in a half nod while digesting the story. In another second, great sheets of skin on his face would rise up, turning his eyes into slits and exposing teeth set wide apart by the long, slow jaw growth of the disease that did him in. He'd peer at you above his glasses and deliver a big, booming laugh.

This was the closest thing to joy I ever saw in Ronnie. Most of his customers bored him. His face fell or kept the same

"oh crap" expression when most of them walked through the shop door. But when they or I made a sarcastic comment he admired, he'd close his eyes in smart-ass authority and pronounce in a rich bass, "Shee-IT!"

Soon after I reconnected with Ronnie, I wanted to write about him. My folks and I had treated him badly. I couldn't fix that. But through him, I thought, I might reveal a lifetime's reach of suffering for a woman and her unwanted child.

THE MORNING I got the call that he was gone, I drove in from out of town. I tore down the interstate as if a magnet in my blood were pulling me back to Ronnie.

At his two rented rooms, his heaps of stockpiled clothes, guns, cash, and food testified to his reclusive life. He'd always been ready for a quick getaway. I'd stopped by to grab his prized camel-colored suede coat along with a favorite shirt, tie, and fresh khakis for the undertakers. I picked a pair of size 14 shoes from a mound of them. At fifty-five, his feet were still growing.

Ronnie's death certificate listed the cause as a heart arrhythmia brought on by a rare disfiguring disease. More than anything, however, Ronnie's distrust of people killed him.

Once, he'd been a sweet-faced little boy with soft gray eyes and white-blond hair. Pictures show him giggling as a baby and, up to the first grade, beaming like a handsome prince. Then his circumstances took an awful dive. Ronnie lost his base of support. He was thrown from one institution to another. In early adulthood, he won his freedom and achieved some small-town dignity. He made friends and had some fun. Then biology would take its turn clobbering him.

Old driver's license photos reveal that in his twenties a glandular disorder began transforming his face, hands, feet, heart, larynx, airways, gut, all his insides. Over decades, it turned him into the freak he always thought himself to be.

He avoided stares by getting his food at drive-throughs. He thought he was just turning old and ugly earlier than most people. Maybe he looked like his father, he said, whoever the hell his father was.

It occurred so incrementally that it would be decades before anyone on his short list of friends realized something medically terrible had been happening to Ronnie. They'd witnessed it, yet they hadn't understood what they were seeing. His girlfriends drifted away as he became sicker and stranger looking, and I came back into his life too late to make much of a difference. No one—not his doctor, not his dentist, not the men who sat in his chair for their flattops and their high and tights—not a soul had sounded an alarm insistent enough to help Ronnie save himself.

Now his young doctor appears by my chair at the casket. I rise to stand beside him. Shoulder to shoulder, we gaze silently at Ronnie. We had tried hard to help. There was a way, but it required more self-love and more faith in people than Ronnie possessed.

THE DAY I learned that Ronnie had died, our mother suggested we cremate him. It didn't seem right to me to shove him in an incinerator. We settled on the casket and a graveside service, with a couple hours' visitation the night before. She would pay for it all. After lying about Ronnie all his life, it was the least she could do.

Our mother was a different person to each of us. To me she was as loving as she could be. She tenderly nursed my fevers. She cheered me when I was down. Every day for decades, no matter what city or country I was in, I found a phone booth and called her. She gave me everything she dreamed of for herself: unending love, summer camp, piano lessons, college, store-brand clothes. Ronnie got none of that.

My tenderhearted mother grieved when Daddy cleaned out nests a bird kept building in her newspaper box. She befriended lonely old ladies, and she loved nothing so much as holding a baby. How, then, had she turned so cold toward her firstborn?

THE DAY BEFORE the funeral, she and Daddy arrive. She is anxious and grumpy. Ronnie's death has chased her out into the open. I listed her in his obituary. "He is survived by his mother, Adria Bishop . . ." She doesn't say it, but she probably wishes I hadn't. I know she's relieved that nobody back in her town will see it. They don't know about Ronnie.

Ronnie's customers and neighbors begin to shuffle by his body for the visitation. We're in the funeral home's smallest room, so we're jammed in close. His landlord tells me Ronnie ached so deeply that he impatiently cursed a young waitress at his favorite home-cooking place. He felt bad about it, so forever after he insisted on sitting in her section and tipping her well.

A customer reveals that Ronnie was too weak toward the end to walk even a single block to deliver his barbershop rent. Ronnie gave the guy a free haircut for walking his money up the street.

The next morning, at Ronnie's grave, the undertakers escort Mom, Daddy, and me into wobbly chairs on the cemetery's uneven ground. Mom's cousins and lifelong friends stand in a semicircle behind us. They grew up with her and are some of the few people who ever knew she had a little boy named Ronnie. I don't see any tears in her eyes, but I put my hand to my mother's back. The gesture feels false, but I leave it there.

THE YEAR BEFORE he died, Ronnie was rushed to the hospital in respiratory distress. I was with him every day for the next five weeks. More than once, he nearly died.

Doctors asked me to go to his home and bring back his identification cards, insurance papers, and clothes for his eventual release. His landlady unlocked his upstairs door for me. Slung over a piled-up chair were the slacks he'd worn the last day he'd worked.

I found his wallet in the right back pocket. I extracted his current driver's license, and it was then that I found, tucked behind, five others spanning twenty years. I had stumbled across an unintended record of his disease's march across his face. I was about to bag it all to take to the hospital when I noticed something in his left rear pocket.

I fished out a tight stack of greeting-card-sized papers, each folded over once. The little sheaf was bundled in two directions by ten or more rubber bands. Some were new. Some were medium fresh. Deepest down, bands were brittle and broken with age.

He had transferred this precious packet from pants to pants like a talisman. He'd been sitting on it atop his barber's stool for years.

I teased apart the compressed papers. A bank stub was on top. Beneath it were two birthday cards decorated with pictures of butterflies and taffy-like candies. An Easter card of pastel flowers. A letter. Some pieces of correspondence were four years old; one six years old. The postmark on one had eroded away.

In them, the writer asks Ronnie how he is and chitchats about vacations and Halloween decorations and strep throat and grass mowing and a cataract surgery. Penned inside a birthday card, "Can't you come over for lunch Sunday? We would love to have you! I'll bake you a birthday cake."

"Do come and see us soon—call so I'll have something decent to eat 293–4823," read another.

Ronnie jotted that number on other papers in the stack, preserving the digits as if they were a lifeline to be tapped in case of emergency.

Each piece of mail is signed with the two words that, in spite of everything, brought comfort to Ronnie:

Love, Adria

Losing the Mother I Thought I Knew

Mom at about sixteen.

After Ronnie was gone, we stuffed the awkwardness about him back under the family floorboards. Mom lived fourteen years more, and tensions surrounding Ronnie's life troubled our relationship to the end.

I'd press her gently for information on her first pregnancy and her on-again, off-again times with Ronnie. My curiosity irritated her, but sometimes she'd offer up a tiny detail, like how baby Ronnie had a cold the day the social worker took him to his foster parents and how Mom worried about him all that day while she worked. I'd tuck scraps of their story into my journal.

After his death, I learned he left no will. His medical debts

far exceeded his savings and his tiny bit of life insurance. Someone needed to sell his cars, guns, and barber chairs and to distribute those assets to his creditors. Arthritis and early signs of dementia made it impossible for Mom, at seventy-five, to do it. It would have been too emotionally painful for her anyway, and besides, she lived a hundred miles away and didn't drive. I lived just across a mountain valley from Ronnie's place. I could do it, and I wanted to.

LATER THAT YEAR, I went to Mom's town and drove her to a notary public at her bank so that she, as Ronnie's next of kin, could legally transfer the estate job to me. "I am the mother of Ronnie Lee Overstreet..." Mom handwrote on her engraved stationery. It was the first time she said it straight out, on paper.

She was nervous as we headed to the bank. Might the notary know her? Might her carefully kept secret seep out into her longtime home of Charlottesville, Virginia?

The notary was a stranger. Mom was safe. Wrinkles in her brow smoothed away as I drove her home.

IN 2002, SHE and Daddy moved to my street in Roanoke, Early Bishop, Virginia, two hours from Charlottesville. My father died of emphysema eight months later.

The following year, at eighty-eight, Mom broke a hip. Her arthritic knees stymied her rehab. She was stuck in a nursing home because she couldn't get out of bed and stand on her own.

She rarely mentioned Ronnie by name, but I knew she was thinking about him. Out of the blue, she lamented to me that

she was no good, that she had sinned, that she was unforgivable. Nothing I said eased her mind. Was she grieving over how Ronnie's life had gone? Or was she still stuck on the fact that she wasn't married when she had him? Maybe it was the simple fact of Ronnie's existence that hounded her. It was hard to tell.

I wrote a letter, marked "confidential," and left it at the office of her compassionate new minister. I told him that Mom had been bearing a shameful lie nearly all her life and shared her secret with no one. I told him what I knew about Ronnie. Unable to distract herself with much of anything, Mom was finally alone with her terrible sense of unworthiness. She was fretting over her very soul.

One day when I was out, the minister came to Mom's room and prayed with her. Without letting on that he knew her secret, he did his best to shore up her faith in God's forgiveness. No end date on it; nobody was ever disqualified, no matter what. A few weeks later, on an early spring afternoon in 2005, her heart very slowly stopped beating. She died nice and easy.

OF ALL THE virtues in Mom's value system, "pretty," which she pronounced "priddy," was close to the very top. So, the day after she dies, I arrange the prettiest two-city send-off she could have imagined.

THE MORNING IS mild, with the smells of warming earth swirling all around us as my husband and I drive over the Blue Ridge Mountains for Mom's church funeral and her burial in the cemetery on the mountainside near Thomas Jefferson's

Monticello. I'm wearing the blue moonstone necklace my mother wore on her wedding day.

The three years I looked after her have been hard. No matter how much I tried, I couldn't bring her peace. I couldn't make her happy with herself.

All that heaviness weighs on me, yet the funeral turns out to be a lighthearted homecoming. Mom's friends, nieces, nephews, former coworkers—they're all there. The prettiest flower arrangement, in fuchsia, orange, and gold, is from the rich boy she raised as a nursemaid on his parents' country estate. Two ministers celebrate her life, along with Daddy's, that sunny day. One of them draws a comic hoot from the crowd when he says that Daddy, a die-hard Democrat, is the only person he ever knew who voted for Michael Dukakis.

Just as with Ronnie's service, nobody mentions the single greatest burden of my mother and my brother—her shame over having had him out of wedlock. It wouldn't be appropriate to bring it up, of course. Most of the funeral crowd has no clue about Ronnie or, when it comes right down to it, any of my mother's private concerns.

BY THE TIME Mom dies, most of her closest friends are gone, so I don't hesitate to list Ronnie in her obituary in Charlottesville's newspaper, the *Daily Progress*.

A few minutes before the funeral in the chapel of Mom's longtime church, Anna, daughter of one of Mom's dearest, departed friends, motions for me to come to her in the front pew.

"Mary Carter," she whispers, her voice full of concern as I bend my head to hers, "there was an error in the obituary. It says she had a son. Adria didn't have a son."

A "hate to break it to you" look emerges on my face, and Anna lifts her head in surprise. "Did she?"

I'm standing five feet from the open casket, where Mom is laid out in the last piece of clothing she purchased, a white silk jacket embroidered with pink and turquoise butterflies. I nod to Anna.

Anna digests this, then asks, "My mom knew, right?"

Anna's mother was as understanding as anyone Mom ever came across. She radiated empathy. If she'd learned Mom's secret, she would have embraced Mom all the more. But I shake my head. No, she never knew.

A DOZEN DAYS after the funeral, I dream that I'm standing downhill from a just-felled tree when it begins to roll. It's too big for me to jump over and too long for me to run around.

BACK HOME, I began to sift through the things Mom and Daddy had brought to the little house down the street from us. Mom couldn't bear to throw much away, so from their old house I'd carted Grandma's cast-iron lard-soap-making tub and Daddy's grain-musty burlap feed bags. I'd boxed up drawers full of paper scraps and little keepsakes that, though she didn't often look at them, gave my mother great comfort. Now I was opening them up again. Many days, I sat cross-legged on the floor by Mom's living room recliner. Her curly silver hairs drifted from boxes and fell to the carpet as I sorted through it all.

I found notes from her throughout. "The little hat I wore when we were married 1942," she wrote on a torn piece of envelope placed over the flattened hat of silk flowers.

"Mary Carters [*sic*] baby clothes" was on an index card atop a pink-and-blue blanket, embroidered little dresses, flannel gowns, and white leather baby shoes.

"The white hat with roses I wore when Mary Carter finished college" was attached to another squashed hat.

"Buttons for Daddy's Harris Tweed sports coat," she'd written on a paper scrap in an envelope with the leather buttons, as if she meant the note for me. She'd been so proud she could buy him such a classy jacket.

I kissed the old church bulletins and magazine clippings about African violets as I dropped them into the recycling box.

Just as Ronnie had done, Mom wrote her new address and phone number on stray paper napkins, receipts, and business cards. Uprooted from Charlottesville, she needed to be ready when somebody called and wanted to know where she was. She wasn't always sure.

Crying out from the piles of hand-copied recipes and bus trip brochures and yellowed, perfectly ironed white linen napkins was what she wanted most for everyone to know: Adria Bishop tried to be good. She was a responsible woman. She was well behaved, an upstanding citizen.

I recognized this demonstrative clutter from somewhere else. Ronnie left behind a similarly intentional mess. Among the Hardee's wrappers, I had found receipts for laundered towels for shaving customers long in their graves, dealer sales slips for a long line of used cars, and tax scribblings from the mid-twentieth century.

But I was determined to push behind these facades. In my mother and my brother, I'd witnessed a connected misery. They were entwined in a dark and irresolvable way. They could neither be close nor break free of each other. They were

anxious and self-doubting, in much the same way. I wanted to know what happened to them all those years ago, why they'd wandered off from each other.

I needed to know why my mother had let Ronnie suffer when I had it so good. I wanted to be able to fully love her again, and to understand what it had meant to me, always sensing her shame and only recently learning clues to its origins.

I began to track my mother's history and Ronnie's. He kept everything. She kept everything. I kept what they kept, and I was a reporter. I dug into the poverty of Mom's upbringing and the extreme wealth of the place where she had come to work as a young woman, the old plantation where I'd grown up as a servant's child and where she and Ronnie lived together the longest. The landed gentry there played a role in Ronnie's story, and I researched the individuals who sent him off to his final institution.

I raced to interview elderly people who knew Mom or Ronnie. I mined thirty years of my journals and indexed the thousands of pieces of their stories. I pulled together documents from the orphanage, the reform school, and the mental hospital that all had detained Ronnie.

He never knew his father's name. I found that name long after Ronnie and Mom were gone, and I went looking for the man.

This book grew from a decades-long effort to shine light on the darkest corners of my family's life, to dwell in the contradictions of the relationship between my mother and her secret son. The story of my mother and my brother, and the private shame they shared, is also the tale of the cruel world that shaped them. Their story sheds light on the difficult, punishing mores of the American South in the twentieth cen-

tury. In these pages, I consider our lives and the society that made us who we all were. I did my best to move beyond the whisperings and the lies and the expectations of a culture I cannot condone, yet it haunts me still. I am left to tell the story in all its complexity.

WITH A MAGNIFYING lens one afternoon, I was studying photographs from Mom's first months with baby Ronnie. For her camera, she posed him on blankets in the grass and on chairs out in a yard. From one album, I pried a small picture of Ronnie at almost five months old. He's on a wooden bench outside in a sweater, diaper, and leather booties. He's squinting in the sun.

On the back of the picture she'd written, "Sweetest thing on earth."

PART II

THE PARENTS

WHO RAISED ME

My Mother: Gentle Hands and Foul Moods

Mom, Daddy, and me at my uncle's house in
Northern Virginia when I was about a year old.

My mother's hands made my life. They churned our butter, kneaded our biscuit dough, checked my head for fevers, delicately plucked gravel from my knees, and when I had a cold, dabbed the medicinal reek of Vicks VapoRub on my chest from the cobalt-blue jar. At her side in church, I'd twirl her wedding rings around her finger and play with those soft hands. On long rides home from out of town in the farm pickup, I'd sprawl across her wide lap and doughy body. I lounged on her as if she were my couch.

Adria slowly made a bright home out of the weathered

century-old place we got to live in when my father became manager of the farm. As Arthur Godfrey plucked his ukulele on the radio atop the fridge, she bleached cotton feed sacks in a big tub outside the open back door and sewed them into coarse, heavy bedsheets. She dyed some of those sacks red to fashion my red-and-white Mrs. Claus costume for the school pageant. I feared the other farm families like us in the audience would recognize the humble cloth and look down on me.

She'd often be reduced to dimes and nickels, but she was too proud to admit it. We'd hide in the bathroom and cup our hands over our ears as salesmen peddling brushes or vanilla extract pounded on our door.

My second-grade teacher sent word home that I couldn't read the blackboard and was holding books inches from my face. The eye doctor prescribed glasses and a yolk-yellow liquid vitamin A in a dark-brown bottle. Every evening Mommy faithfully fed me a teaspoon. She and Daddy struggled to pay for it. I craved the stuff and can remember the taste even now. She kept it on the fridge's top shelf, out of my reach, and policed that precious potion so as not to waste a drop.

She was my nurse and my guardian, my manners coach, my hairstylist. But only rarely my playmate. Except for my first rolls of a ball and for her storybook readings as I fell asleep, she never played with me. I was her beloved project. Her job was to feed, clothe, and protect me, not to entertain me. Her nervous, chicken-blinking blue eyes were forever turned in my direction.

IN THE BACKYARD one warm evening before supper, Daddy was helping me learn to walk along the top of the three-board

fence that separated our yard from the cow pasture. I envied the nimble fence-walking of other kids. Daddy, once a dare-devil boy, was lightly touching my outstretched hand as I stepped foot over shaky foot on the narrow board. "You're doing good, Pie." That was his nickname for me, short for Sweetie Pie. "Don't be scared. You're gettin' it."

Out the back door and down the steps Mommy flew. "Mary COD-ah! Get down from there right now! You're gonna fall down and break your neck!" (She said that often.)

Daddy shook his head. "Swee-dart, you worry too much. She'll be all right. Let the child *play*." She'd squelched my other athletic efforts—tree climbing, balancing at the edge of brick walls, and pumping myself so high in my swing that I almost flew backwards over the tree branch that held it.

I crouched atop the fence, deciding whether to defy her. She'd shaken me up. I'd surely lose my balance now. Finally, I crawled down and slinked away, pouting. I never learned to walk a fence.

DREAD OF COMING disaster ruled my mother's life. She never learned to drive, but from the passenger side of the truck, she squealed whenever Daddy approached an intersection or when vehicles shot past us. "Earl-LEE!" she'd scream my father's name in a crescendoing screech. "Watch *OUT*!" Her right foot wore a hole through the truck's floor mat from slamming into her imaginary brake. Each time before we went out, she'd park herself in front of her electric stove and intone, "Off-off-off-off-off," pointing to each switched-off burner knob, plus the oven's, to be sure.

In a crowd, Adria Bishop, at five foot eleven and nearing

two hundred pounds, was almost always the biggest woman. She stood erect with long, spongy arms and legs. She was curvaceous, with a narrow waist. Warm when engaging with people, on guard and blinking the rest of the time, her expression oscillated between welcoming and forbidding. Her brown hair was thick, permed, and sprayed.

She hated her body and compared herself unfavorably to the highly polished rich women who lived all around us. She fetishized their sharply defined Achilles tendons and bony ankles; her own lower legs were thick and fleshy. She thought her breath was foul, so she sucked cloves. She asked me all my life, "Does my breath stink?" It never did. Her bodily fluids repulsed her, so even when she wasn't having her period, she kept wads of toilet paper in her crotch. They would fall from her underwear and scatter along our floors, trailing her quiet shame. She found herself so odious that she feared her very biology might contaminate us.

For some reason, my mother needed for me to be very well behaved. At church, she held rule over the Women's Circle like a stern, stiff-backed Puritan. There, she always wore her finest, putting on the most upright costume she could scratch together—a hat and a suit, if she could, with a broach at her high collar. At home, she could be jovial, bordering on bawdy, though when I was nine she warned me fiercely, "Don't you ever let a boy put his thing in you."

The tender side of her pitied the sparrows that stunned themselves by flying into her windows. She placed them high on a ledge, away from cats. But her moods could cloud easily. Often she'd stew all day over something, her face in a childish pout. If some woman irked her, say, by asking her to bring a pie to the church picnic when she'd just baked cookies for it,

she took strong offense. "Tough tittie," she'd grumble under her breath.

She cried a lot of angry tears throughout my childhood. Many times I'd find her weeping alone in the kitchen, her face red, puffy, scary mad. She and Daddy had just exchanged words; about what, I didn't know.

I thought she was nuts. Her extremes made no sense. I had no idea how deeply tormented she was, or why.

My Father: Joy, Wonder, and Self-Hate

My aunt shot this picture of me, Daddy, and
my little cousin in the mid 1950s near backyard
outbuildings at our house on Bridlespur Farm.

It's the picture I prize above all others. Mommy took
plenty of us, but only on Sundays, when we were dressed
up, when she felt the proudest of us. My Ohio aunt took this
one of me and Daddy as we were most of the time. Looking
at it, I hear the crows cawing across the hills; I smell the
dusty hayfields that separated us from the mountains; I feel
my father's affection in the squeeze of his strong, callused
hand.

We're in our backyard, out by the ham house and the tool-
shed. I'm about eight. I'm in a Saks Fifth Avenue bathing suit
tossed out by our boss lady. Its breast cups collapse onto my

bony chest. I'm standing between my little cousin and my ball-cap-wearing daddy, who's in khakis soiled by farmwork.

When my father wasn't baling hay, wrangling a bull, or doing something else unsafe, I was out on the farm with him or riding beside him in the pickup. He was my fellow explorer, my gentle teacher, my playmate, my partner in fun and wonder.

Not long ago, the rustle of a brown paper bag in an adjoining room lit up a delicious association I didn't know was still lodged in my mind: That sound meant Daddy was home with a bag of Atomic Fireballs and little Tootsie Rolls.

He'd invite me to pull his earlobe, and after a few tugs, he'd bare his teeth, shake his head ferociously, and bellow like a beast. He'd slip his arm up his jacket sleeve and tell me to stick my hand up the dark tunnel at the cuff where he claimed a mouse was in residence. His hand would pinch mine; I'd shriek, and we'd do it over and over.

When he found a rusty tricycle so old the tires had rotted off, he coiled baler twine around the wheels for my bumpy rides along the farm roads. He hammered straight the mangled rails of a discarded sled and, taking a running start, sailed down a snowy hill in a solo ride to show me how. He sheathed his comb in waxed paper and hummed "Jimmy Crack Corn" into it, harmonica-like. On the Fourth of July, he parked Mommy and me on a dusty road below the bosses' country club so we could watch their fireworks from the back of the pickup.

Daddy introduced me to wildness. Back by the mountain, he plucked persimmons for me, golden and tart, and chuckled when my mouth puckered. He explained the strength of tall pecan trees we watched in a hurricane, their giant crowns nearly bending to the earth but the trees not breaking. And he

opened my eyes to the profusion of smaller plants that crept over every uncultivated inch of the farm.

"People fuss about dandelions and wild onions, but Pie, look here." He ripped away a honeysuckle vine invading his squash patch. He cast his flat hand high above the garden's edge. "We got sand briars over there. You know, those little thorns that stick in your feet? Here's some plantain, and look over here." He pointed to wild violet leaves that had lost their purple-and-white blooms. "See how the earth is determined to cover itself?" If weeds weren't covering the ground, the rains would wash the soil down into the creeks and the rivers and be gone. We'd be down to bedrock with no soil in which to grow our cucumbers and strawberries or to feed the livestock.

As farmers' tractors mow the fields and till the earth, they routinely kill wild creatures. Most farmers scoff at the unavoidable slaughter, but my father mourned the rabid opossum he mercy-shot as it hissed at him through foamy teeth. Many an evening, he came to the supper table, his head hung low. In cutting tall hay, he'd sliced into a nest of baby rabbits he couldn't spy in time to swerve away. Like my mother, my father grieved openly when animals died.

He named his female hound Sam Catchem after his favorite detective in the *Dick Tracy* comics, and he called for her with a whistled melody learned from his father—the climactic passage of *Messiah*'s "Hallelujah" chorus, though Daddy didn't know that's what it was. Sam was a runt weeded from the private pens of hounds carefully bred nearby to run alongside horseback foxhunters. Daddy snapped her up as a pup. She was his sidekick as much as I, and she was smart. In killing the groundhogs that devoured Daddy's crops, she avoided their

long incisors by grabbing them first by the tail and spinning them until they were so dizzy she could then attack them head-on.

Before his question-mark-shaped spine began to collapse and shorten him, Early Lee Bishop was a handsome six-foot tower of tanned strength, with soulful down-turned eyes. A bitter whiff of his sweaty, hay-covered forearms drifted to my nose as he swung me around. His pack of unfiltered Camels made a crushing sound within his shirt pocket.

I had no way of knowing it then, but he was my first and finest instructor in journalism. He trained my eyes and ears to teach me that there are no truly ordinary people or places, not anywhere, not ever. If you listen closely enough, if you watch carefully enough, you can be astonished by every square foot of this earth.

He tuned my ear to the poetic phrases of everyday life, and as we drove on errands into the narrow farm lanes off the main highway, he showed me the history of our county, settled by the English almost three centuries earlier. "Pie, see how the banks right here are high?" He braked the pickup to a stop, and I glanced beside us at the five-foot-tall roadsides lined with old cedars. "That means it's a really old road. Wagons wore it down, through years of mud and ice and horse manure."

For his true-life tales, usually featuring hapless country people, he used a primitive palette of description from the backwoods where he'd grown up. You could smell the oily scalps. You could hear the mouse's dying squeaks. You could taste the red dust. Daddy stretched my imagination every time he opened his mouth. He possessed the curiosity of a sociologist, the empathy of a pastor, the sensibilities of a poet. But he didn't think so. He was optimistic about everything but himself.

Most of us shrug off the little mistakes, but my father saw each one as proof of his incompetence. He misspelled a word on a note to his boss. He dropped and shattered a light fixture at the big house and was therefore hopelessly clumsy. He kept saying "pacific" instead of "specific" in his Sunday school class.

While Mom's self-hatred centered on her moral worth and her physical features, his was aimed at his intelligence. Though they were constantly affectionate toward me, together, my parents made our house a year-round festival of self-contempt.

The love between them flickered like a dying porch light. Lovey-dovey when with company, they whispered furiously while at home, and their struggle bewildered me. They seldom argued outright. They stewed; they glowered; they sulked. She adored him and longed for more of his tenderness. He rebuffed her mostly, though he did thank her for grooming him as if he were a child. She combed and parted his hair, laid his church clothes on the bed, served up sixty years of nourishing food. Yet he didn't seem to respect her. She lacked his patience in doing things. She rebelled against recipes and instructions. She dripped paint on the wood floors. When she took black liquid shoe polish to his scuffed brown shoes, he shook his head and walked out of the house. But even as a child, I knew there was more to this story. There was something larger for which my father blamed my mother.

PART III

OUR WORLD

The Kingdom of the Rich

Mom took this snapshot of the main house at
Bridlespur Farm around 1940, shortly after her
arrival and its construction.

My parents arrived in Keswick, Virginia, as young
adults, each with good reason to feel unconfident.
As it happened, they landed in a place that wasn't inclined
to think much, either, of people like them. They were servants in a kingdom of the rich.

In 1940, Mom came to the country crossroads of Keswick,
in Albemarle County, and to Bridlespur Farm to be a nursemaid for a rich couple's baby boy. Daddy, a young farmhand
on a nearby estate, fell in love with her and soon went to work
in Bridlespur's fields and barns. They would live there for the
next forty years.

As a little girl, I played office with the slick annual reports of major corporations in which the bosses owned stock. I played dress-up with a black satin cocktail hat adorned with the long feathers of a tropical bird. Our bosses' castoffs became my playthings.

From our house, in the middle of hayfields, we could see three mansions in the distance. The heirs of great American fortunes were scattered about the neighborhood—Pillsbury, Anheuser-Busch, du Pont. Wealthy people had been flocking to Keswick for hundreds of years, each taking their turn at playing lords and ladies of the manor.

In recent years, I dug into the history of Albemarle County and confirmed what I sensed to be true back then. It never was much like other counties. Albemarle's settlement by Europeans in the early eighteenth century wasn't so much by scrappy frontiersmen who crafted rough cabins with their own hard hands. There were some of them, sure, but the people who laid down the dominant culture were the sons of affluent English-descended coastal tobacco planters looking for new fortunes inland. They sent their slaves and overseers ahead of them to tame the wild territories and to set up great British-style estates. The stunning geography finally led the aristocrats to move in and to stay.

At the dead center of Virginia, Albemarle is lush, green, and beguiling. Three-thousand-foot peaks of the Blue Ridge rule the county's northwestern corner. If you were to fly southeast from there, you'd see green hills rolling softly through the county seat of Charlottesville and Thomas Jefferson's "academical village," the University of Virginia. Just before the Blue Ridge topography submits to the Piedmont's lumpy plains, it spits out the low-slung Southwest Mountains.

Jefferson's Monticello sits on a knob at the southern end of the mountain range. In the first half of the eighteenth century, his kin and family acquaintances began snapping up royal land grants for land stretching from his birthplace at Shadwell to the hamlets of Keswick, Cismont, Cobham, and on up the twenty-mile chain.

Tobacco wound up degrading Albemarle's rich soil, so the gentry began to grow wheat, grapes, and apples, as well as the county's reputation as an oasis of fine living and low taxes for ladies and gentlemen. In Keswick, they set about re-creating English high society, complete with foxhunts, trumpeting brass horns, and a scarlet-coated master of the foxhounds. The new American squires gave their estates names reminiscent of the old country—Cloverfields, Merrie Mill, Castle Hill, Merifields, and my personal favorite, a later one, Tally-Ho.

My section of Keswick sat between two parallel entities: the mountains to the rear and, out by the farm entrances, Virginia State Route 22, a winding two-lane road that had been Jefferson's carriage route to Washington. Between the road and the mountains lay vast side-by-side plantations, and on each one, a minor fiefdom consisting of a large main house, tenant cottages for workers, and enough outbuildings to look from the mountaintop like a toy farm set. There were stables, barns of all kinds, chicken coops, meat-smoking houses, horse-riding rings, springhouses, silos, miles of white-painted fence, and all of it surrounded by velvety, unspoiled hills. Keswick was British nobility in miniature, and like all the upstairs-downstairs servants who trimmed the boxwoods, poured the highballs, bleached the linen, and made the little crustless watercress-and-cream-cheese sandwiches, my parents were extremely cautious around rich people.

With most kinds of work, there's at least a little buffer between the laborer and the employer—a union, a human resources department, maybe some midlevel supervisor. But with us, the ratio between Daddy and job security was one-to-one. Our housing, our food, our electricity, our transportation, Daddy's small monthly check—it all depended on the favor of his bosses. One rash move and they'd put us out.

I WAS A baby in a carriage when Mommy began shushing me as we neared their house. Later on, when I could walk, I'd toddle beside her down the long farm road. I'd wave to Daddy and the other farmhands in the fields. I'd squeal with glee at the horses, the cows, the sheep, and the dogs.

If I was still carrying on as we approached the big house, Mommy would jerk my hand hard. "Mary COD-ah," she'd warn in a threatening whisper, "you be quiet. You'll wake them up." Our bosses, who'd never worked for a living, slept late. I was not to kick the gravel, laugh, shriek, or in any other way behave like a normal child around the big house. I came to associate wealth with punishing authority.

It may seem strange—I'm in my seventies; I graduated from an Ivy League university; I've worked in big cities—but the drawn-out, entitled voice of a rich Southern woman, a voice that takes its time because it can and because it's accustomed to getting its way, to this day can stop me cold, can nearly paralyze me and render me mute. A few years ago, I confessed this to an elderly African American woman who spent her life cooking and cleaning for the wealthy. I told her I was still scared of rich white people. She shot back with a fierce eye: "You better be."

I REMEMBER STANDING in our front yard as foxhunters on tall steeds paused at a gate to Bridlespur's back acres. The creak of polished boots, gloves, and saddles; the jingle of bits and stirrups; the horse snorts visible in the chill morning air—a hunt was an impressive production. Groomsmen back at each rider's stables spent hours polishing leather and braiding tails and manes before the hunt. Five feet above my young head, the party of men and women in tight-fitting riding clothes chattered on, literally above it all. They didn't notice me. I studied the lean and glamorous women—their bone-handled crops, their neatly netted chignons just below their velvet helmets, their perfect lipstick and pancake makeup. I felt sorry for the overburdened horses of the fattest men, who also seemed to be the meanest with their whips as the horses stumbled under their weight.

Often when I went with Daddy to the Keswick post office for our mail and the bosses' and to pick up groceries at Morris' Store next door, those same jowly, red-faced men would be lounging beside their wood-paneled station wagons, loudly and drunkenly holding forth. I saw them too when my folks and I sold coffee, hot dogs, and bottles of Pepsi under the grandstand at the Keswick Horse Show as we raised money for a community center. It's no wonder I came to think of Keswick as a beautiful, ugly place.

Daddy told me that my impression was extreme, that not all Keswick people were arrogant. It's true there was a well-off woman who sent bags of hard candy and oranges every Christmas for children at my school. And she, or someone else, donated books awarded every spring to the best students.

My all-white Cismont School, in use since 1908, still had outhouses and potbellied stoves when Ronnie went there in the forties and I in the fifties. To reduce dust and soot, teachers kept a coat of oil on the wood floors of the classrooms. At home, mothers rubbed their fingers raw scrubbing our greasy skirt hems and the boys' grimy pant legs. My best friend's mother fretted to our principal that her first grader might slip through the hole in the girls' two-seater Johnny house. School officials had no money to build indoor toilets, so they simply plopped regular wooden toilet seats over the holes to shrink the openings and keep the tiniest kids from sliding into the muck.

Four teachers taught seven grades, with all but one of them doubling up, two grades each. It was the age of ballpoints; our wooden desks still had holes for inkwells. The frame building's upstairs auditorium was off-limits for fear its squeaking floor would collapse under our weight. Black schools suffered even more. All this was particularly galling in a county that in 1960 ranked number one among Virginia's rural counties with the greatest number of high-income families. The affluent people of Albemarle County sent their children to private schools, often in far-off places. In my childhood, when the county's middle class was still tiny, the millionaires dragged their feet about raising taxes to upgrade the antiquated public schools for the rest of us.

When Daddy became our PTA's president, he commiserated with the county school superintendent about the conditions. The man wept as he told Daddy about the plea he'd made to the county's governing body, the board of supervisors: Albemarle's horses had finer quarters than its public school children.

TO THIS DAY, drivers along Keswick's picture-postcard Route 22 catch a glimpse of Southern grandeur from centuries ago. Across thousands of preserved acres, they see highly bred horses munching fescue from within white-painted fences, and long, cedar-lined driveways leading to manor houses secluded in groves of tall hardwoods. The charming tableau is backed in the distance by the long expanse of softly rounded mountains. Off the side roads, however, there has always been another story.

Keswick's social structure cut three ways in my time: First came the upper class, with their estates, country club, golf course, foxhunting club, quaint stone Episcopal church, and rollicking social circuit. Then came the white servant class, living either in tenant houses on the farms as we did or in small homes far off the picturesque highway. We shared a school, a Presbyterian church, and a women's home demonstration club, an offshoot of the county agricultural extension service, where Mom learned to sew my school jumpers from patterns. The third sector, the most crucial workforce and the most poorly paid, was Keswick's sizeable black population, clustered in modest homes on the back roads, with their own proud society of small schools and churches. For seventy-hour weeks in 1940, a black Keswick chauffeur earned less than my farmhand grandfather did for sixty hours, and my grandfather was blind.

Slaves built Keswick's grand homes and made Keswick the handsome, fertile place it continues to be. In 1840, Albemarle County slaves outnumbered free people of both races. Hundreds of slaves once worked on the plantations nearest

my home. The history is rich and fraught. Descendants of en-slaved carpenters and stonemasons constructed architecturally charming houses for themselves, but in my time many other black men and women subsisted in shacks hidden in the woods. As I was writing this book, a few elderly African American women were still cooking and cleaning for white people, some-times for offspring of the original boss and occasionally in the very same mansion. A few years ago, an eighty-four-year-old woman was keeping house part-time for descendants of the family she'd first gone to work for at the age of ten.

Out among whites, black servants were exceedingly quiet and careful, and for sound historical reasons. In 1910, eight leading citizens of Keswick accused a visiting black clergy-man of being a "race agitator." They beat him with riding crops and barrel staves in the presence of his black hosts and set him on a train out of there. Keswick's black elders have long been intensely tight-lipped. Their guarded tongues were a blessing for the elite because Keswick has long been a hedo-nist's playground.

To earn extra money, Daddy parked cars for soirees at Bridlespur and other farms. The rich men liked Daddy and slipped him five-dollar bills when he pulled up in their valet-parked Rolls-Royces and Packards after parties on some-body's terrace. Daddy helped clean up the party mess later and would come home chuckling about the panties he found snagged in the boxwoods.

Many estate owners didn't have jobs and never had. Their surroundings were sensuous, natural, and luxuriously private. They could spend their days chasing after foxes and their nights chasing each other, and occasionally their servants. Publicly upright, privately naughty—that was Keswick's reputation.

Writers, movie stars, and aristocrats had long sojourned there. In 1955, twenty-three-year-old Elizabeth Taylor and co-star Rock Hudson filmed farm scenes for the movie *Giant* a five-minute drive from Bridlespur. William Faulkner rode on Keswick foxhunts and sipped liquor at local parties. Decades later, I sat near area resident Sissy Spacek in the waiting room at Mom's orthopedist and stood beside Ann Beattie as we both picked up clothes at Brown's Dry Cleaners in Charlottesville.

As a kid, I watched the big shots' parties only from a distance. Late on a summer night, I could hear laughter and big-band music down by the bosses' pool. When I squinted, I could make out the torches in the gardens and the movements of couples in cocktail attire. Just up the hill from our house, I once observed a uniquely Keswick kind of party, though I only watched the parade of luxury cars gliding by us on the farm road, and later, from our front porch, I heard the distant merriment. On summer Saturdays nearest a full moon, farm owners still take turns hosting a traditional monthly hill-topping. They have their farmhands mow a scenic hill and invite friends to drive there, circle up, and serve fine foods from the trunks of their cars. They feast on shavings of country ham, sip fine bourbon, tell bawdy stories, and carry on half the night.

Ronnie was bolder than me. As the hours crawled by, people usually became so drunk they didn't notice him. He crept right up and snuck a ham biscuit when he could. He watched from woods near the Keswick country club's golf course one night as a young married socialite, naked, engaged in a drunken orgy on the ground with University of Virginia fraternity boys. He turned the sprinklers on them before bolting back into the darkness. Eventually, Ronnie would pay dearly for his snooping.

The People in the Big House

Anne and John S. McIntyre Sr., at their cold-
weather retreat in Winter Park, Florida, 1939.

When my folks interacted with their bosses or any
other people of means around Keswick, I'd watch
their faces take on a childlike docility. They lowered their
heads and their voices, like children braced for punish-
ment. It distressed me, and shamed me. Why were they so
extremely deferential around more powerful people, even
their young doctors? Why did their quick yes-ma'ams and
no-sirs seem so reflexive to me?

In midlife, I began to make sense of their sheepishness.
Both their fathers had lived and farmed on the land of more
affluent people. My parents grew up in subservience. At one

point, my dad's dad was booted from one of the estates, leaving his wife and seven children in the extreme pinch of poverty. On Daddy's mother's side, her brother toiled in Bridlespur's fields years before Daddy got there. And far from Keswick, in more modest rural communities, Mom's cousins labored for better-off people. I came from a long line of servants.

By the time I transferred to the county high school, most of my Cismont School friends had left the farms. Their parents had landed more independent jobs in town. Because Mom and Daddy remained on Bridlespur for four decades, their sense of dependency soaked longer in their consciousness.

A HUNDRED YEARS ago, my Granddaddy Bishop was known around Albemarle County as a gifted orchardist. Landowners hired him to look after their apples, peaches, and grapes. When Daddy was a boy, Granddaddy lamented to him that he felt unappreciated. He longed for his bosses to come down from their manor houses and stand with him among the trees. He would show them how he banished this worm and that mold, how he preserved tender blossoms under a threat of frost.

But the owners, not ones to get their hands dirty, remained aloof. They might house Ed Bishop and his brood in one of their workmen's cottages for a time. They might thank Ed after a bounteous crop of Black Twig and other vintage apples. But few cared enough to witness his science and his art.

A few years ago, I found an entry in my journal about that little long-ago scene between my father and my grandfather. What Granddaddy said that day resonated in so many ways within my family dynamics.

"I'm like the fly on the ox horn," he told Daddy. "Don't know when I'm there. Don't miss me when I'm gone."

The metaphor of a vulnerable insect dancing for attention on a beast's unfeeling, unyielding horn would stay in Daddy's mind over his lifetime. He would often think back on his father's loneliness and feel his own in a county where you were either poor or rich, with few people in between.

EXCEPT FOR MY Granddaddy Bishop, most of my kin's bosses were actually not much more prosperous than they were. For my parents, however, the asset gap zoomed from thousands of dollars to millions when, in the 1940s, they settled down to work for a du Pont heiress and her husband, the son of a Midwest hardware tycoon.

Anne Andrews McIntyre's grandfather was Eugene du Pont, third-generation executive of the DuPont chemical empire and, until his death in 1902, patriarch of one of America's richest and most powerful families. When Mom first met her, Anne was twenty-four and resting at her in-laws' estate outside Roanoke, Virginia. She'd just given birth to her first child. Anne's mother-in-law had asked other wealthy families about nursemaids and found my mother, then single, twenty-two, and longing for more stable employment.

Anne had attended Sidwell Friends in Washington, D.C., the Quaker school favored for the children of presidents and other national power brokers. She completed her education at a finishing school in Florence, Italy. The year before Mom connected with her, Anne had married John Sharpless McIntyre at the du Pont family's ancestral place of worship, Christ Church Christiana Hundred in Greenville, Delaware. Buddy

McIntyre, as he was called, was the son of John Joseph "J.J." McIntyre, a bombastic Cleveland businessman who made his fortune in automotive bushings and bearings. J.J. moved his family to the Virginia countryside in order to raise horses.

It was at a horse show deep in the Virginia mountains that Buddy met Anne, a petite, auburn-haired socialite. Like Buddy's parents', Anne's parents kept a stable of fine horses; she and Buddy were both ribbon-winning show riders. Buddy, also in his early twenties, was polished, somewhat shy, with slicked-back dark hair, suave in the manner of a young Richard Rodgers. Around the time of their wedding, Buddy bought Sunny Side, an old Keswick plantation and one-time inn. Buddy and Anne were staying hours away at Buddy's parents' house as their ten-bedroom mansion was being built to replace Sunny Side's rotting one. They renamed the farm Bridlespur.

On my mom's first night at the elder McIntyres' place, Hobby Horse Farm, Anne instructed the cook to fix a supper plate and send it up to Adria's room. Jane Byrd McIntyre, Buddy's mother, intervened. No, she insisted, Adria Overstreet, the only white female in their house staff, would eat downstairs at the dining room table with the McIntyres. Later on, when Mom traveled with the baby to Anne's parents' plantation at Somerset, Virginia, Mom ate in the kitchen with the other servants.

The McIntyre grandchildren called Jane "Nano" and J.J. "Dompy," and my mother did too. Nano bonded right away with Mom as they doted on newborn John S. "Buddy" McIntyre Jr., an adorable child with big brown eyes and bright-red curly hair. Eventually, Nano would become Mom's principal ally in dealing with Ronnie, her secret son stashed off in another place.

Anne McIntyre, stylish striver in Virginia's horsey high society, never pretended to be the mothering type. She left that to Adria, who'd been hired before to care for other babies as their mothers recovered from childbirth. Mom often told me about the time when Buddy's diaper leaked as Anne held him, and she dropped him to the floor. Adria scooped him up. She acted as a second mother to him for the rest of her life.

A few years after the diaper incident, not long after Mom met Daddy, they were heading down a Keswick side road one night in his Willys sedan one night to visit friends. Anne and Buddy, out partying too, pulled their car up to Early's for a chat. Anne mentioned that she'd left little Buddy locked up alone in the house. Mom politely wished her bosses a good night. When they drove out of sight, she told Daddy to turn around and take her home. She retrieved Buddy from the mansion and took him along to their friends' house.

For seven years, Mom tended full-time to Buddy, then to his little brother, Byrd. She left Virginia for the first time when she traveled with the boys to their grandparents' luxurious winter homes in South Carolina and Florida. Once the Bridlespur house was completed, she settled into the cramped maid's quarters, up a steep, narrow stairway above the kitchen.

After Mom and Daddy's courtship and marriage in the early forties, the McIntyres hired Daddy as their farm manager. Their primary focus at Bridlespur was their stable of American Saddlebred show horses, not far from their back door. They handpicked horse trainers and groomsmen and worked in close collaboration with them. Daddy raised the hay, gathered horse manure from the fields, and tended to incidental horse needs, but mainly he cared for the farm's hundreds of back acres, the part of the farm of least interest to

the McIntyres. They rarely walked or even drove to the luscious majority of their land. Their eyes glazed over as Daddy proudly reported how he'd saved the life of an ailing lamb, shot the weasel killing the chickens, or repaired a worn-out hay baler to save them money. They did want him, however, to make sure that the fields looked gorgeous from the highway and from their terrace when they held cocktail parties.

The bosses prized the yellow-green moss on the brick walkways of their formal gardens. To weed the moss before a party, Daddy would get down on his hands and knees, his left hand palm-down on the bricks, with tiny moss-embedded weeds sticking up between his fingers. He'd carefully pluck the weeds to protect the delicate moss. This took hours away from the cattle, the sheep, the fence repairs, and everything else. Daddy sulked as he did it.

But he was as willful as his bosses. He snuck around to practice the humane agriculture he thought right. He once told Buddy Sr. about a sickly calf, refused by his mother. The boss said to kill it. Daddy hid the calf in a back field, and when a neighbor complained about it bawling, the boss said again, kill it. Daddy put it in a barn and bottle-fed it Pepto-Bismol to ease its indigestion. It grew into a fine steer, eventually earning the boss, who didn't know one bovine from another, $1,700 at the stockyard.

This stealth warfare went on between Daddy and the McIntyres for decades. They cared more about their horses and their French poodles than the farm itself, and that fact churned Daddy's insides every day. He once told a neighbor, "It's a terrible thing to fall in love with another man's land."

Daddy baled hay. He milked cows, and pulled pregnant heifers out of ditches in the middle of the night. He cleaned

the swimming pool, hauled trash, and unstopped plumbing in the big house, no matter the hour. He fixed the water pump, took the I. Miller heels into town for a resole, ferried the mail, and shuttled the maid and the laundress in and out.

He tended to Anne's hundred varieties of roses. When they developed canker, a fungal disease, Daddy researched it and advised her to cut the plants back. No, she said, and don't spray insecticides on them either. So in a show of aggrieved servitude that may have gone unnoticed, Daddy lay on his back for days and painted each stem with fungicide. After his death, I found in his leavings a copy of her talk to a garden club about the history of her rose garden. She made no mention of Daddy.

Every winter as a child, I'd ride along when he delivered pickup loads of firewood to the saddest of Keswick's black homes, where alcoholism slowed the lives within and cold winds whistled through the thin walls. Daddy did this for twenty years, until Anne McIntyre found out. She ordered him to stop. She insisted he give her the proceeds from any wood gleaned from her property.

My father never explained that the wood was scraps—worm-eaten fence posts and fallen trees he'd cleared from back on the mountain—and that he gave it away. It was rough, half-rotten chunks with only enough BTUs left to keep a family from freezing for a few days. Nothing like the handsome seasoned oak logs he artfully stacked by Anne's fireplaces.

In most matters, she, more than Buddy Sr., was boss. Anne was smart, determined, exacting. Nearly always done up in stockings and high heels, she spoke with a protracted nasal whine spliced with the entitled drone of the Duchess of Windsor. (Behind her back, Mom called her Annie Poo to mock her

queenliness.) Anne always paid me kind attention and praised my good grades. She gave me a monogrammed sterling silver compact when I finished high school, and when I applied for my first newspaper job in Richmond, she or Buddy Sr. called their old friend the publisher to put in a word for me. Still, Anne intimidated me. I'd never been the target of her demands, but I saw what that was like. I did, though, admire her longhand's artfully interlaced letters, and I still have some of her penciled notes to Daddy: "Early, please bring over some pretty wood 18 or 20 in long so I can lay a pretty fire in the master bedroom— Thanks Mrs Mac—Would like it before 10 a.m."

When her mink coat went missing from her boudoir, she quizzed the black maid, who swore she didn't know where it was. Anne remained suspicious. Later on, she asked Daddy to investigate a stench. Turns out, a sick opossum had climbed through a vent and, in clambering indoors, pulled the coat down behind some furniture and died curled up in mink.

Our house was furnished with the McIntyres' fancy trash. When Anne became convinced that aluminum pots caused dementia, she gave their entire set to us. Mom cooked with those thick pans for the next fifty years.

Daddy rummaged through everything the McIntyres sent to the burn pile or to the mountain trash pit. He salvaged and fixed hundreds of things for us, some of which I still have: broken chairs, a desk, a shoehorn made from an antler, a trash can with a clipper ship on it, a brass letter opener from a busted office set, a fine-bristled shoe brush, a lighted art deco makeup mirror.

Daddy's biggest prize was a Patek Philippe men's watch tossed out when it quit running. Decades later, when my folks moved off the farm and made the acquaintance of a jeweler,

Daddy asked him to fix the Swiss watch, which the man said was worth $8,000. Daddy bragged about it to a younger man he didn't know well. Soon after, someone broke in my folks' bedroom window when they were out one night. The thief left behind a trail of snuffed matchsticks and stole only the watch.

Every fall throughout the fifties and sixties, Anne sent word that Mom and I could come help ourselves to clothes she was sending to the annual SPCA thrift sale in town. Had Mom been a small woman, she would have worn the clothes. But she was much taller and half again as wide as Anne, a frequent shopper at Bonwit Teller, Bergdorf Goodman, and other expensive New York stores. So until I outgrew them, which I did by my midteens, I got Anne's clothes.

Mom and I would feast our eyes on the bounty heaped on the McIntyres' long dining room table: alligator purses, cashmeres, chiffons, and tweeds still exuding Anne's perfume. We ran our hands down the silk linings. Pulled zippers that purred. Snapped handbag clasps over and over to hear the amazing muted *phlumpt*. Marveled at buttons heavier than silver dollars. Imagined our bodies, if they were suntanned, toned, lotioned, and powdered to perfection, slithering in and out of those dresses.

We trudged the long gravel road toward home, my skinny arms embracing scarves and dresses. Mom's strong arms held suit jackets and coats, her wrists encircled with purse handles. We walked silently, quickly, self-consciously, in case Anne might have just gotten home and be spying out a window and think we'd taken too much. Or the poorer hired help might be watching from a barn or a field and envy us. Or maybe somebody would think we were stealing. We definitely didn't

feel worthy of these rich-lady clothes, and I was too young for them. But Mom would lengthen the sleeves and the hems, and I wore the Lord & Taylor coats to church.

FROM THE NEWSROOM of the *Philadelphia Inquirer* one afternoon in July 1981, I made my usual call to Mom. Just a routine check-in. As soon as she heard my voice, hers turned grave. "I have something to tell you." When she was this solemn, she had major news to share, and it usually wasn't good. I'd been at the Jersey Shore the week before. She hadn't wanted to spoil my vacation, so now she was laying it on me. Two weeks earlier, Anne had fired Daddy. I began to sob.

Buddy Sr. had died of emphysema in 1978. A year later, Mom, Daddy, and I stood on Anne's mossy patio and watched her marry a Missouri packaging company executive. They continued to live at Bridlespur. Daddy kept trimming the grass on John McIntyre's grave at Grace Episcopal Church in Cismont. When Anne threw out John's monogrammed mirrored trash can, a copy of his father's photo portrait, and other McIntyre things, Daddy gathered them up for Buddy and Byrd.

Anne didn't care much for my father. She was known as a flirt, and my father's proper Presbyterian-elder demeanor made her uncomfortable. Finally, she got rid of Daddy.

Her new husband did the firing. He insisted that the job was too hard for my father at sixty-three. He noted that some of the Aberdeen-Angus beef cattle had developed pink eye, a common infection. On the farm and at the big house after that, Anne avoided Daddy as her new farm manager took over and Daddy tinkered on the outskirts, trying to be useful. She

sent word through her husband that my folks could stay in the tenant house until they found a new place.

I went back to the farm to help my folks pack up the farmhouse. While Daddy was gathering his tools at a barn, Anne and her husband eased by in their car. When they turned around, Anne waved from the passenger seat. I dug my hands deep into my jeans and glared at her. I felt defiant, rude, a little bit brave.

Daddy had no pension. His Social Security payments were going to be low because his wages had been low. Furthermore, Social Security exempted farmworkers and domestics until the fifties, so the McIntyres hadn't paid into Social Security for either of my parents during their first years of service. Anne offered Daddy a hundred-dollar-a-month retainer for fourteen months in case her new manager needed advice on the big spread. Later on, after Buddy Jr. and Byrd appealed to her, she sent Daddy a check for $8,000, and the boys sent more.

ON MY DRIVE into the farm that July evening, I choked up as I looked around at the evidence of Daddy's handiwork—the fences and gates, the tidy white-painted barns and sheds, the bridge he built between the sheep barn and Anne's rose garden, the fields so rich that an agriculture professor brought students there to sift the fine soil.

When I pulled my Volkswagen Beetle up to the house, my folks were sitting on the front porch in the twilight, waiting for me. Daddy usually worked until nightfall. Mom weeded and harvested in their garden out back until it was too dark to see the sweet peas. It was rare to see them sitting together on the porch.

That night we silently looked out across the hills. We listened as a quail in the tall grasses called its name, "Bah-ob WHITE! Bah-ob WHITE!" We surveyed the beauty that had been ours on a daily basis and soon would be gone from us. As night fell, I glanced down the porch and saw Mom's lower lip trembling, her eyes brimming with tears. Each night that week, the three of us lined up in porch chairs and cried softly to ourselves. I gave up mascara.

Our misery lasted just a few months. My parents bought their first home, in Charlottesville, near their new church and a bus ride from Mom's new medical school job at the University of Virginia. Daddy went to work at the farm supply where he'd been a customer since he rode a wagon there with his father.

AT CHRISTMASTIME IN 2000, Anne was dying in a Charlottesville hospital. She was eighty-six. Her designer dresses had been replaced by hospital gowns. Her reddish French twist was gone forever. She was bald and weighed a mere eighty-five pounds.

Buddy Jr. rushed in from his Mississippi home. Hospice nurses told him she was near death but hanging on. She wanted to see someone, but they couldn't figure out whom. Buddy thought it might be her husband. He'd just had back surgery and hadn't seen Anne for days. Buddy brought his stepfather to her. Anne still wasn't satisfied.

Buddy had witnessed a dramatic change in Anne in her last years. Once a tigress, insistent on things being done her way, she was now gentle and patient. She thanked him repeatedly whenever he came. She had never been so humble,

so thankful, so sweet. Then it dawned on Buddy and Byrd that maybe she wanted to see Early. They said his name, and she perked up.

The day before New Year's Day 2000, my eighty-one-year-old father was home watching TV. Buddy called. He was coming over. He thought his mother wanted to see Early. Daddy pulled on his shoes. Mom grabbed his jacket and pulled its sleeves over his thin arms. At the hospital entrance, Buddy slipped Early into a wheelchair and rolled the crumpled little man to Anne's bedside. She stared straight ahead with her eyes half-open. Hospice nurses assured Buddy she was aware and could hear quite well. Buddy left Anne and Early alone.

Early, the venerable Presbyterian, knew just what to do. He took Anne's thin hand in his still-strong ones. He gently squeezed it. "Don't you worry," he whispered close to her ear. "We're still friends. Everything's going to be all right."

He bowed his head near hers, closed his eyes, and softly prayed that God would take care of his old friend, that he would bring her peace and comfort, ease her suffering, and let her know that all her sins were forgiven. She was as loved as any other child of God. "In Jesus's name we ask it," my father said, as he always closed his prayers, "amen."

Buddy drove Early home. When Buddy returned to his mother's room, the nurses reported that she was finally at peace. They predicted that she would die by sunrise, and that's just what she did.

PART IV

THE LIE

Original Shame

A 1941 portrait of my mom around the time she
became engaged to Daddy. Near the end of her life
she thought she looked sad.

Years later, when my parents, too, were gone, it came
time for me to weave together the fragments of Mom's
life story that I'd been collecting for years. Some of it she
told me. Some of it I never asked about and still don't know.
Some pieces came from her oldest friends and from my re-
search. Here, then, is what I know.

On January 5, 1916, in Moneta, Virginia, a community of
humble farms and rusty gates set along dirt roads, three coun-
ties southwest of Keswick, Adria Lavonia Overstreet was
born.

When baby Adria arrived, tall, pigeon-toed Milton Emmett

Overstreet and his wife Sarah Carter McLain Overstreet already had a ten-year-old son and weren't expecting more children. Carter, as they called her, was forty, so they were surprised when she became pregnant after so long a pause.

A farmhand in a long line of farmhands, Granddaddy possessed a forlorn, elongated face and a tender heart. He whistled so shrilly through his front teeth as he talked that I kept forgetting what he was saying, what with all the hisses and trills. He was twelve when his mother died. By fourteen he was living and working on a neighbor's farm in Moneta. The next year, his father died, and orphan Emmett—with his possessions tied in a red bandanna—showed up looking for work at the Hicks place, run by matriarch Fannie Manning Peters Hicks. People called her Manning.

Manning took skinny young Emmett under her wing, and soon he was singing in the choir at Bethlehem Methodist, the church she'd helped found. Manning possessed such righteous faith in the Lord that on a scorching, cloudless Sunday during an extended drought, she brought an umbrella to church, explaining, "Well, we're praying for rain, aren't we?" At twenty-nine, Emmett married slender, gracious Carter McLain, so well respected that just their engagement brought him up in the world. Along with Emmett's maternal granddad, the couple moved into a rented farmhouse near the Hicks spread.

In those early years of the twentieth century, few people in Moneta were truly rich. Moneta was an agrarian hamlet in highly agrarian Bedford County, with not a lot of fanciness about it. Today Moneta is part of a resort community built around the five-hundred-mile shoreline of man-made Smith Mountain Lake.

In Granddaddy's day, it was plain, unassuming countryside, and farmhands like him worked for people just a social notch or two above them. The Hickses owned land and had far deeper resources than the Overstreets. Some of the Hickses became bankers, accountants, teachers, and engineers. But Emmett went to the same church as his bosses and ate corn bread and beans just like they did. They got along like family. They'd make a party of shelling together the black-eyed peas they'd dry for the coming winter.

Just as Daddy was everything on Bridlespur, Emmett was *the* man on the Hicks farm. He raised their main crop, chewing tobacco, or as Mom always said it, "tuh-BYE-kuh." He plowed the thousand-acre Hicks farm with horses Prince and Lucy, hollering "Gee!" to go right and "Haw!" to go left. Among hundreds of chores, he grew the fruits and vegetables, raised the chickens, milked the cows, maintained the Hicks house, and hooked the horses to the buggies for Manning and the lady schoolteachers who boarded with her. Before dawn on school days, he rode alone on a horse through the quiet fields to light the fire in the schoolhouse stove.

Like an all-hours towing service, Emmett and the horses pulled wagons, then cars, out of ditches. When Hicks family members left Grandma Manning's house in foul weather, he'd hitch a mare named Old Nora to a buggy and follow them on the muddy road until they reached a more solid one. Granddaddy loved the Hickses.

People at Bethlehem Church embraced long-necked layman Emmett with his oversized ears and oversized suit, but they groaned whenever he launched into one of his long-winded, lunch-delaying prayers. Years later, when they remodeled the sanctuary—using timbers from Manning's farm—they told

him they found some of his benedictions still flapping around in the rafters.

He was a sweet-natured hick, usually in bibbed overalls, with a toothpick parked behind his ear. He brought his live chickens by train to sell at the Roanoke farmers' market, where I still buy homegrown spinach and kale. Emmett was so polite, he'd tip his straw farmer's hat to every person he passed on Roanoke's busy streets. To be sure he didn't miss the last train to Moneta, he kept an eye on the Elgin pocket watch tucked in a special pocket of his bibs.

I WAS IN my thirties before Mom filled me in on the first really bad thing that happened to her. On a Tuesday evening in September 1920, she was four years old and riding along with her parents to revival services at Bethlehem Church.

The headline of a yellowed newspaper clipping taped to a sheet of paper stuck in Granddaddy's Bible announced it: *Woman's Neck Broken.* The *Bedford Bulletin* reported two versions they had been unable to reconcile: One was that the horse pulling Carter and Adria's buggy ran out of control. Emmett, in another buggy in front of Carter's, managed to stop Carter's horse as it passed. The sudden halt slammed Carter against the wooden dashboard, snapping her neck.

The other account had it that Emmett, Carter, and Adria were in the same wagon when their horse and another behind them started to run. In that version, Emmett, an expert buggy driver, stopped his horse suddenly and got out to quiet the second one. When he reboarded his rig, he found Carter slumped over, nearly dead. "It is said that she breathed only a few times after her husband found she was hurt," the newspaper reported.

I cried for my poor traumatized mother when I learned this. No wonder her startle response was set so high. No wonder she kept warning me that if I wasn't careful, I'd break my neck. She watched her mother die that way. Mom would never fully trust the world again.

When the whole countryside gathered at Carter and Emmett's house that evening to comfort Emmett, they found the green beans Carter had snapped that morning for canning. Her house was so orderly it was easy for them to tend temporarily to Emmett and the children.

My mother lived with a memory of her father lifting her mother from the buggy and laying her on the ground. Adria always wondered if in moving her, her father inadvertently brought about the fatal injury to her spine.

Manning Hicks, sensing the need for long-term motherly oversight, invited Emmett, Adria, and Adria's brother, Clarence, to move from their rented farmhouse into a log cabin across the yard from her spacious white farmhouse.

Fourteen months after Carter died, Emmett married curly-haired forty-year-old Annie Belle Preston. It was her first marriage, and people continued to call her Miss Belle for the rest of her life. She and her father, Jesse Preston, moved into the cabin. With stone chimneys on each end, a tiny living room and kitchen downstairs, and two little bedrooms upstairs, it was tight quarters for five people. After Mom died, I stood at those chimneys, all that remained of the house after a long-ago fire, and picked up a stone to keep. I could imagine everything Mom told me that happened there.

She and Miss Belle clashed immediately. Miss Belle had little patience with children. She forced Adria, only five years old, to haul heavy buckets of water from the creek and to

collect and squeeze to death the grotesque green worms on the tobacco plants. The slimy yellow innards were smeared across Adria's clothes.

My mother grew into a long-legged mischief. Miss Belle insisted that she wear scratchy brown wool stockings to school until June every year. So Adria pulled them off in the woods and put them back on before she got home.

When Miss Belle farted, she'd confess, giggling, "I pooted." My mother was ashamed to be associated with her. She sassed Miss Belle. She snuck up behind her and threw a slimy eel around her neck.

One summer afternoon, Miss Belle stretched out on the cabin's cool kitchen floor and fell asleep. She had one knee propped up, and her wide-legged underdrawers gaped open to reveal her genitals. Adria felt pure disgust course through her. She grabbed a pepper shaker and doused Miss Belle's labia like a pan of raw chops headed for the skillet. Miss Belle awoke on fire and chased Adria around the farm for an hour before coming home to tend her red-hot crotch. When Adria grew hungry that evening and crept into the house for something to eat, Miss Belle beat the crap out of her. The war was on.

Adria grew into a tall, curvaceous dark-haired beauty with big, sorrowful gray-blue eyes. Emmett had adopted Manning's moral code: No card playing. No dancing. No makeup, except the purple juice of pokeberries for women's lips. No liquor, except for Mr. Preston's hidden-away medicinal hooch. No taking of the Lord's name in vain. No hanky-panky of any sort. And practically nothing besides breathing on the Sabbath. Adria was about to burst out of her restless skin.

At Christmastime in 1934, she was only eighteen, but being sullen and shapely and tall, she looked older and far more

worldly than she was. Adria was giving Miss Belle some lip one day when Belle's cousin Dessa was visiting from a distant town. Belle had had enough of Adria's mouth. She sent her home with Dessa until after the holidays.

RODESKA "DESSA" KRANTZ Miller, widow of a railroad conductor, lived in Covington, Virginia, a sulfur-reeking pulp-mill town in the mountains of western Virginia. Covington and nearby Clifton Forge swarmed with railroad men and with loggers who trucked timber day and night to the pulp mill. Dessa's life was much more lively than Adria's back in Moneta. At Dessa's, people drank liquor, danced, and played cards.

They did all the things Emmett Overstreet didn't allow. But Emmett and Miss Belle didn't know that.

At Dessa's, Adria was negotiating life as an adult for the first time, and she was extremely naïve. One night at Dessa's, a man considerably older than Mom gave her a beer and led her to a dark outbuilding. She said it was the first beer she'd ever tasted and her first intercourse. The man was married and already a father. I don't know if she'd ever seen him before.

Over the years, when I'd talk with Mom about that encounter, I tried to define it as a rape, but she never felt comfortable with me using that word for it. "It was my fault," she told me many times. As far as she knew, the man never found out he'd gotten her pregnant, and she was glad for that. "I never wanted to make trouble for his family."

In Mom's oldest albums, I found a picture of Dessa's daughter sitting beside a man on a leafy bank, but the picture was torn in half with just the man's pant legs, white socks, and

dark shoes showing. Could Adria have ripped away the image of the man who changed her life?

I've tried hard to identify him. Mom would never tell me his name. She knew I'd snoop around, and she didn't want to take the chance of dishonoring him—even though, of course, he had dishonored her. Ronnie never asked her who his father was; he thought she might not know, and he didn't want to humiliate her.

But after Ronnie and Mom died, I found the man's name on documents from two institutions where Ronnie lived as a young boy and as a teenager. Mom, always compliant with authority figures, dutifully provided the man's name when Ronnie was admitted to each place. I wish like hell I'd learned that name while Ronnie was alive. We could have worked together to learn about the man. In deference to Mom, I'm not naming him.

His name is neither the most common nor the most unusual, along the lines of a James Goodman or a William Lawson. No one by his name appears in documents at the county courthouse in Covington. Census records coughed up more than thirty men with that name scattered around Virginia. After eliminating those who were nonwhite, had no children, or were children themselves when Mom got pregnant, I zeroed in on a railroad brakeman who died more than thirty years ago. His railroad line was along the Virginia coast, on the other side of the state from Covington. Still, I thought maybe he'd been passing through. I'd confirmed that a brakeman by another name was friendly with Dessa. Maybe that man was railroad union buddies with Ronnie's father.

At long last, a couple of years ago, I located the niece of the brakeman's second wife. I'd already learned a lot about

him. I knew that he was born in North Carolina and that he lived in the Virginia state capital of Richmond nearly all his life. His son had cerebral palsy and died in his thirties. His second wife was an ex-nun. Maybe the reason Mom made no demands on this woman's uncle was because she knew about the disabled child back home. I wanted so much for this man to be Ronnie's father. I knew so much about him. I could solve the mystery once and for all.

I waited expectantly for his niece, Kathy, to email me pictures of the man. My heart fell when I saw them. He was handsome, in ways entirely different from Ronnie. His face was round; Ronnie's was long. His mustache and eyebrows were dark and curly; Ronnie's stubble and barely visible eyebrows were blond and straight. Chin, nose, eyes, ears, mouth—no resemblance whatsoever. Sometimes children do look nothing like their parents, but in this case, the match simply didn't seem possible.

Covington is only about fifteen miles from the West Virginia state line. So next, I focused on West Virginia men and eliminated thirty-one more with that name. But who knows where the man was from. And was that his real name anyway? I'm still looking for him.

WITH FEW CLUES about the early signs of pregnancy, Adria came home to Moneta after Christmas without a care in the world. She celebrated her nineteenth birthday four days after New Year's. But by spring, she knew she was in trouble. Her condition was obvious to her father, her stepmother, the Hickses, and all Moneta. Her best friends' mothers no longer allowed their daughters to be seen with her. She'd dropped

out of high school before graduating. Where could she go? Times were hard enough already. Her father had just cut three fingers off his right hand while cutting logs on a saw rigged to a Model T.

Never one to meddle in female affairs, Emmett longed for the wisdom of his first wife, Carter. He didn't know what to do with Adria, and pressure was mounting to drive her out of Moneta. Emmett had a brother nearby, but he had nine children, and they were so poor that when blizzards approached, the kids frantically plugged mud between their cabin's logs so they could sleep without the snow falling on their heads. Finally, the lady organist at church suggested Adria go to the Florence Crittenton Home, a shelter for unwed mothers and their babies, in nearby Lynchburg.

For more than a year, Adria stayed at the Crittenton Home, a large brick house in an old neighborhood. She knew no one in Lynchburg. The woman from her church was one of the few people, maybe the only one, who ever came to see her. Stern female wardens lorded over the girls, who were poorer, coarser, and wilder than Adria. She kept mostly to herself. When the time came for her delivery, two policemen drove her to the hospital, as if she were a criminal.

Her labor was difficult. Doctors used forceps to draw out the baby's head, which left it temporarily misshapen, but there was no mention of brain damage. Eight-pound Ronald Lee Overstreet was born on August 27, 1935.

In those early thirties, women smitten with debonair English movie actor Ronald Colman named their sons after him. The "Lee" in Ronnie's name, of course, was for Confederate general Robert E. Lee—a hero to millions of white Southern-

ers. Thousands of people born below the Mason-Dixon Line still carry the middle name of "Lee."

On the back of a picture of baby Ronnie, Mom wrote his birth date and "Ronald Lee Smith." His birth certificate already said "Overstreet," but she still was deliberating what last name to give him, and even for her private purposes, she chose a generic. Eventually, she gave him hers.

A mother and her baby could stay at the Crittenton Home for a year after birth. Mom took courses in nursing and mothering. She learned how to care for her little boy. She fed him a lactic acid baby formula, considered then to be more modern and dignified than breastfeeding. By all accounts, including Mom's, Ronnie was a darling baby with eyes like hers, the color of blue-gray slate. On his first birthday, Mom took a picture of him on the grass in the home's yard, his hair tenderly wetted and parted by her.

People at the home must have talked with her about giving Ronnie up. Later on, when a couple wanted to adopt him, Mom wouldn't agree to it. For a while, at least, she was determined to be Ronnie Overstreet's mother.

On Her Own

On Ronnie's birthday, Mom dressed him up
and parted his hair before shooting his picture,
probably in the yard at the home for unwed
mothers.

Worry, along with a young woman's heady optimism, thrashed within my mother late in the summer of 1936. Her and Ronnie's year at the Crittenton Home was up. It was time for them to leave and make room for the next wave of mothers and babies. She was twenty and Ronnie was one.

With a list of hiring services for domestic workers in her pocket, Mom brought Ronnie to Roanoke, the only city of any size in the rockier, poorer, more mountainous western half of Virginia. It was a good place to start over.

Set in a green valley where the Alleghenies sidle up to the
Blue Ridge, Roanoke was close enough to country to feel like
home but teeming with people hard at work at the Norfolk and
Western Railway and the world's largest rayon plant, American
Viscose, known to locals as the "silk mill." Families streamed
to fairs and movie houses and variety shows Mom had never
heard about in little Moneta. Among all those strangers, Mom
could get a fresh start.

She was free from the prying eyes of the strict matrons
back at Crittenton, free from Moneta's judgments of her as
that fallen Overstreet girl, and thank God almighty, free at
last from Miss Belle. But times were tough, the Great Depres-
sion was at rock bottom, and my mother knew no one in
Roanoke.

I never learned where they stayed at first, maybe in a
boardinghouse, maybe at the Salvation Army. In her initial
jobs, she cooked and cleaned in homes. Then she hooked up
with a Roanoke agency that, for a fee, connected her with
people needing practical nurses to care for new mothers and
their babies and for people dying at home. In those years,
women stayed in the hospital for a week after giving birth,
then were on bed rest for days at home. Any family who
could afford it hired a girl like Adria Overstreet to come
take care of the mother and baby. But for Mom, there was no
child care and very little temporary housing or other help.

All my life with her, whenever any complications, whether
medical or financial, were mentioned concerning a newborn,
Mom would say reassuringly, "Every baby brings its own
welcome." But there was no welcome for Mom and Ronnie.

Someone who knew Mom told me that without anyone to
care for Ronnie while she was on a job, Mom took him with

her to a customer's home. She needed to leave Ronnie and go across the house to do her work, so she pinned him in his diaper to a bed so that he wouldn't roll onto the floor. She must not have been able to hear him wherever she was on the property, but his shrieks of frustration alarmed the residents. Someone alerted the authorities about this unmarried girl and her suffering baby.

Late in her life, I asked Mom what happened. "Did you really pin him to a bed in his diaper?" "No!" she replied angrily, frowning at me. She knew who'd told me, and she knew that person wasn't likely to have manufactured something as bizarre as pinning a baby to a bed. Her voice grew quiet as she thought back to 1936. "I don't know. Maybe I did." Then her voice became softer yet. "I don't remember much about back then."

A "field visitor," an early type of social worker, took charge of Ronnie. In her late twenties, with a flapper's wavy brunette bob, the woman quickly lined up a childless couple to be his foster parents, and Mom was relieved. She long kept in touch with the social worker, who sent the gift of a high-chair pad when I was born years later.

ROY HALL WORKED on a Roanoke County dairy farm. He and his wife, Mellie Beal Linkous Hall, a former schoolteacher known as Polly, lived in a tenant house there. They were older than Mom. Roy was around thirty-six; Polly, about twenty-eight. They were unable to have biological children. Ronnie had a cold the day the social worker took him to the Halls. Adria had to go to work and didn't meet the couple immediately. She worried about him all day, but when she met Polly and Roy, she knew Ronnie was in good hands.

Mom rented a room in a twenties bungalow in Roanoke County, just two miles from Ronnie. On days off, Mom walked those miles through farmland to visit Ronnie at Polly and Roy's. She often brought along her Brownie and snapped many pictures of Ronnie. In one taken in winter, Roy, wearing a suit and a fedora, stands in a yard holding little Ronnie as Polly, appearing rigid in dark church clothes, looks on. "Polly, Ronald and Roy," Mom wrote in the photo's top margin. At the bottom, she penned two words with quotation marks around them for emphasis: "*Our baby.*"

From an early age, Mom was an eager picture taker. She carefully preserved thousands of photographs in albums and boxes. In all that trove, I never found a single one of her and Ronnie together. Not once, it seemed, did she hand that Brownie to someone and say, "Here, take one of us."

A procession of boyfriends from that period slouch through her photo books: big old boys in gaudy ties, awkward Sunday suits, farmer's tans, and white socks. Their faces are weathered; their hair, Vitalis slick. As she photographed them, they leered lustfully back at the leggy girl behind the camera.

During her workdays, she was getting a peek at how the other half lived. In Roanoke's West End, she cared for the baby of a grocer who was on the Roanoke City Council. Then a well-to-do Jewish family of scrap-metal dealers needed Mom's help with a newborn son, the care of his mother, and the last days of an elder. Mom was with the old woman when she died. The Methodist girl watched transfixed as the family kept shiva. They turned mirrors to the wall and buried the old lady without makeup, in a casket never open to view. It was all so different from Moneta, where people defied death with pancake makeup on the corpse, cheeks with clown-like circles

of rouge, and lines of wailing mourners filing by open coffins. In 1938, that family recommended her to the McIntyres. Mom expected a short-term hire, like all the others, but she was hoping for more.

WHEN MY MOTHER arrived at Hobby Horse—by city bus or driven by the McIntyres' chauffeur—she would have come up the long wooded drive to the house. This wonderland of Old South high living was like nothing she had ever seen.

Bells of grazing goats jingled in the thick forest below the house. Pastures, berry patches, and apple orchards were set off in the hilly distance. Just outside the house lay a formal English-style garden. Nano McIntyre had engaged a landscape designer to plant more than a hundred English boxwoods and to create ornate iron gates, a serpentine brick wall, red brick walkways, a goldfish pond with lily pads, and a wishing well surrounded by a tall, basketlike metal enclosure.

When Mom stepped inside the house, her eyes must have widened all the more: ten-foot ceilings, shiny oak floors, intricate wainscoting, Persian rugs, ticking grandfather clocks, and gleaming antiques. The living room alone measured six hundred square feet. The place felt more like a hotel than a home.

The staff took her to the kitchen and showed her how a needle on a clocklike device on the wall informed servants which room one of the McIntyres was buzzing from for service. The house was run by a black workforce—a cook, maid, chauffeur, and gardener/handyman. At least one horse trainer, a white man, and often a stable boy were outside with the horses. With Mom, the staff numbered seven.

The rest of the workers lived in their own homes or in the servants' quarters in the backyard. Mom slept next to Buddy's crib upstairs in the main house. The cook, who'd moved with her chauffeur husband from Cleveland with the elder McIntyres, whipped up lobster Newburg and cheese soufflés, the first fancy food Mom had tasted. Mom and the cook listened to gospel music on the kitchen radio Sunday mornings. Years ago, I called another of the McIntyre chauffeurs. When he went off to World War II, Mom wrote to him every week until his return.

Nano, missing her daughter, who had died in childbirth, must have seen something that touched her in Mom. Nano's granddad had owned a hotel in Ohio. She hadn't grown up impoverished, but neither had she been born into the kind of wealth Dompy had built for them. Right away, in October 1938, Nano and Mom bonded in their love for baby Buddy. Nano became like a mother to Mom, and Mom became like a mother to Buddy.

He was different from lean, platinum-haired Ronnie. Buddy was plump, cherubic, with large brown eyes, red ringlets, and a houseful of people showering him with affection. While Adria had struggled to dress Ronnie in secondhand shirts and booties, Buddy came swathed in hand-knitted sweaters and the finest down-filled bedding New York had to offer. Buddy didn't make her feel guilty. This was babyhood done up right.

The earliest pictures I have of Mom and Buddy are soon after Buddy's late-October birth. Those black-and-white photographs are so tiny, I long overlooked the moment of wonder captured there. A bit of window, shutter, and dentil molding in one picture tell me that Mom and Buddy are almost certainly on the lawn at Hobby Horse. The grass has not yet

turned brown and only a few leaves lie on the lawn. Frost has not yet come.

Mom is kneeling beside Buddy, who is dozing within downy light-colored bedding in a low baby buggy. Mom's wearing a warm-looking coat. A silk scarf is tied around her hair and under her chin. Her tender gaze at Buddy and her softly cupped hand resting on the edge of the buggy lend reverence to the scene.

Circumstances prevented Mom from caring for her own child, whose face reminded her of the man who disgraced her. And yet here she was, paid to love Buddy, who looked nothing like her and was three years younger than Ronnie. Her crisp white uniform and white shoes announced to the world that she was the professional nanny attached to this baby. She could love Buddy publicly, wholeheartedly, with pride.

Anne and Buddy Sr. were itching to move into their new Keswick house, designed by an architect who'd worked on restorations at Monticello and Colonial Williamsburg. It was taking a while.

As winter turned to spring at Hobby Horse, Mom settled into the cushioned window seat on the wide stair landing each afternoon as Buddy napped. While she read magazines in the sun, song sparrows caroled high in the forest. This wait was fine with Mom. She was swept up in a movie-like set of glamour. Forget hauling water. Forget tobacco worms and a hickish old stepmother. Mom felt like a queen. She didn't tell anyone about Ronnie. With him safe and far away, she was aiming for a more honorable life for herself, and just maybe, Ronnie could eventually be part of it.

EARLY IN THE forties, Mom and the McIntyres finally moved to Bridlespur Farm. Rich people weren't just here and there in Keswick as they were in Roanoke. Keswick crawled with them. Mom had entered a deeper culture of prosperity. The new house—ten bedrooms, nine baths, eight fireplaces—was larger and more opulent than any place she'd seen.

Pushing Buddy in his baby carriage, Mom began to explore the farm's 332 acres. The two of them would pet the towering horses' velvety noses and peer inside the bustling milk house. They checked out the small tenant house and the larger, more weathered one, empty then, at the far end of the place. Some days Mom pushed Buddy all the way to the foot of the mountains, where farm owners from a century before were buried in a small cemetery, their slaves in unmarked graves nearby.

Mom and Buddy described those early years at Bridlespur as a languid, lovely time. The McIntyres had dinner promptly at seven o'clock. Afterward, on dark winter nights, Mom and Buddy would watch from a window as a lantern's glow slowly approached from the direction of the distant, wooded settlement where a young kitchen servant lived. Her husband was coming across the fields to walk her home. After she'd wiped the last dish, the couple and their spot of golden light slowly disappeared back into the darkness.

Ronnie, Mom's secret boy, was receding from the forefront of her mind. But not for long.

Polly and Roy

Ronnie's faith in Polly Hall is unmistakable
here. His combed hair and clothes show her
attentiveness.

I was growing ever more curious about Ronnie as Mom
lived out her final years, but I held off serious research.
I didn't want to torment her with puzzling details I might
uncover. I'd be too captivated with them to keep them to
myself.

But in 1999, when Mom was eighty-three, my local news-
paper in Roanoke carried a story about the Linkous family. I
knew from Mom that Ronnie's foster mother, Polly, was born
a Linkous. I called a family member mentioned in the article,
and soon I was on the phone with Polly's sister. Polly was in

a nursing home, but at ninety-one, she was still sharp. It was now or never. I had to see her.

Ronnie had been dead almost eight years. He'd described to me how happy he'd been with Polly and Roy. He was sixteen months old when he went to live with them. He believed they were his parents. As soon as he could talk, he called them Mother and Daddy.

On a drizzly January afternoon, I found Polly in a wheelchair off a long hallway at Meadowbrook Nursing Home, between Roanoke and her hometown of Blacksburg. Like most white people of advanced age, Polly's pigment had faded long before. Ivory skin, wispy white hair, she was as translucent as a window sheer flapping in the breeze. Her eyes, however, were startling pops of blue.

"Polly?"

Her eyes searched for me. I took her hand.

"I'm Mary Carter Bishop. Ronnie Overstreet's sister." She let this sink in, then squeezed my fingers. "Oh, my goodness. How is Ronnie?"

I told her he had died. She fell quiet. "I'm so sorry."

I'd brought pictures, but Polly was mostly blind. She couldn't see Ronnie in middle age. Nor could she see how much I looked like him. She strained to hear me. Wax clogged her ears. With her lower teeth and gums collapsing, her little chin rose almost to her mouth.

But when I sat close and directed my questions straight into her better ear, she remembered everything. I visited her four times. Even so many years later, she remained mystified about Mom's behavior toward Ronnie. "It was hard to understand. I felt so sorry for her."

POLLY AND ROY began looking for a child soon after witnessing friends' overjoyed adoption of a little girl. Somebody heard that a social worker had a homeless baby boy. "We said, well, we'd be happy with a little boy." The social worker came to interview them straightaway and in just a day or two, she returned with Ronnie in her arms. It was Christmas, and Ronnie was the best present Polly and Roy ever had.

Because he'd been confined so much during infancy, Ronnie's muscular development was delayed, but soon after arriving at Polly and Roy's, where he could stretch, crawl, and kick to his heart's content, Ronnie began to walk.

For the next five years, by all accounts, he was a contented child. Pictures show him dressed up, grinning behind a big, round birthday cake, surrounded by toys, and scrunching his face in laughter while petting a dog. In my favorite, he stands atop a porch railing, Polly holding him safely around his torso. One of his arms curves familiarly around her neck while the other touches her arm.

Polly's brothers ran three small stores in the New River Valley, forty miles west of Roanoke. Not long after taking Ronnie, Polly and Roy moved to Blacksburg so Roy could work for Polly's brothers and their new family could be embraced by the whole Linkous clan—aunts, uncles, elders, and more cousins than Ronnie could count. Polly had eight brothers and sisters, and a mob of nieces and nephews.

One Christmas when Ronnie was around four, Polly and Roy lined up a spectacular holiday for him. Too excited to wait, they woke him up at two o'clock Christmas morning and announced that Santa had come. Ronnie raced downstairs

to find a Lionel electric train chugging along its tracks and a pile of other presents. It had snowed overnight, so later on, Roy put chains on the car and off they rode to Polly's parents' farm at Merrimac, a coal-mining community on the other side of Blacksburg. Ronnie and all the Linkous grandkids feasted on candy, oranges, nuts, and everything a kid could want. Grandpa Linkous gave him a hand-carved wooden dancing man and the most-prized part of the dinner rabbit, the back.

Ronnie did well in his first year at Blacksburg Elementary. He took piano lessons and voice lessons. Those years were the pinnacle of his childhood. He felt loved and wanted.

People had told me Polly was a rigid fundamentalist Baptist who thought her Episcopalian and Presbyterian relatives were going to hell because they didn't adhere strictly enough to the Scriptures. Maybe she'd mellowed in old age, but she was nothing but sensitive and kind when I was with her. She'd had polio as a child and suffered sickly bouts with arthritis and other ailments throughout her life. Frail Polly may not have been the hardiest or the warmest of mother figures, but she could give Ronnie what Mom could not: her unwavering attention.

Polly's kin were farmers and gardeners. On birthdays and summer holidays, tables were set out in the yard at Polly's parents' house and loaded with ham biscuits, fried chicken, butter beans, and homemade ice cream. Ronnie had a pony to ride, vast lands to wander, and dozens of Linkous playmates.

Whenever she could, Mom visited Ronnie at Polly's house. She'd accompany Polly and Roy when they drove him to Moneta to visit Grandpa Emmett and Miss Belle. Ronnie was their first grandchild.

For the rest of her life, Mom had only good things to say

about Polly and Roy. She would be forever grateful to them. They had embraced little Ronnie when she could not. She warned them, though, that she'd want him back if she ever found a husband.

Early on, Polly and Roy were urging Mom to let them adopt him. Unless they did, they had to run every little decision past her. They wanted to truly be his parents. Mom kept putting them off. But the years were slipping by and she was still single. Polly and Roy grew impatient.

At one point, Polly and Mom arranged for Ronnie to move to another foster home where he would have brothers and sisters. The two women agreed that a larger family might be good for him. Quickly, however, they saw that the mother was favoring her biological children. One night when Polly and Mom knew the woman would bring Ronnie to a church service, they went there unannounced to observe. The woman had laid Ronnie on a pew. Even before he saw Polly, she heard him crying, "I want my mama, I want my mama." He meant Polly, and she took him right back home.

By the 1940s, around the time Mom met Daddy, Polly and Roy were warning Mom that if they couldn't adopt Ronnie, they would have to let him go. "I tried to make her see that she was ruining him by not allowing him to be adopted," Polly told me three years before her death at age ninety-four. "Just kept him all stirred up, all the time."

Roy had gotten a better job—as a fireman at the Hercules Powder Company's military ammunition plant at Radford, Virginia, not far from Blacksburg. He and Polly had the resources now to provide even more generously for Ronnie, maybe even send him to college. Yet they felt no certainty about him at all. If Mom was going to whisk Ronnie away,

Polly wanted to get it over with. But at this point, Ronnie didn't even know Adria was his mother.

ONE EVENING IN August 1941, while Buddy was napping, Mom strolled around Bridlespur with the farm manager's daughter. On their return to the young woman's cottage, a tall fellow was standing by a Willys coupe waiting for her brother to emerge.

Six-foot Early Lee Bishop, farmhand on another estate, possessed the droopy eyes, cleft chin, and hangdog handsomeness of actor Robert Mitchum. He was twenty-three, bashful, and better-spoken than your average hay-bale-slinging roughneck.

Mom, at twenty-five, older and more experienced, accepted his offer of a short ride to the McIntyres' house. She felt an attraction right away. The next day, she couldn't quit thinking about him. He began to write poetry for her. Daddy asked her to marry him that Christmas Eve.

World War II was about to begin, but Daddy was ineligible for the draft and ashamed of that. As a boy, he'd taken a wild ride on a pig that bucked him off in hard barnyard clutter. His shattered right elbow would never let him fully straighten his arm again, and scoliosis shaped his backbone into a question mark. Since he was the youngest of seven children and the last remaining as siblings moved away, it fell to him in his teens to support his mother and his father, blinded now by chemicals he'd sprayed for years in apple and peach orchards. Daddy had dropped out of school. He confided to Mom that he'd always felt inadequate. His mother told him often that he was clumsy and less skilled at physical labor than his brothers. Mom's

affectionate care of Buddy spoke to Daddy's needy soul. He came right out and asked Mom to give him the mothering he'd never had, which, coincidentally, Mom had so little of herself.

Here was a nice man who could make her a respectable married woman. He could provide a home for her and for Ronnie. But that wasn't going to happen anytime soon.

ALL OF A sudden right after Christmas, piercing through the haze of Mom's new love, she received terrifying news: Polly and Roy were giving Ronnie back to her. Mom panicked.

Polly and Roy were at their wits' end. Polly told me they'd rather have buried Ronnie than given him up, but that's what they had to do. They'd been warning Mom for months that this day was coming.

But Mom couldn't very well bring Ronnie to Keswick. She was still living at the McIntyres', still caring for Buddy, then three, as well as getting ready to care for his baby brother. She had no home for Ronnie. Besides, nobody in Keswick even knew she had a son. How would she explain who he was? And who would care for him while she looked after the McIntyre boys?

She reached out to Nano. Mom saw her often, in Keswick, Roanoke, and Florida, and she maintained a daughterly trust in her. Nano, a member of Roanoke's historic St. John's Episcopal Church, calmed Mom and offered to use her influence to get six-year-old Ronnie into an Episcopal orphanage, Boys' Home in Covington, Virginia, coincidentally just a few miles from where he was conceived.

Nano promised Mom confidentiality, even from her own son and daughter-in-law. They eventually found out, but an

early note in Ronnie's Boys' Home file cautioned that Mom didn't want her employers to know about Ronnie.

Daddy didn't know either for the first three months he dated Mom. Finally, with great trepidation, she revealed her secret. "I told him everything," she wrote in her diary, twice underlining those four words. The next day's entry: "Even tho I know I've done right, I just don't know what I will do if early don't still love me." Another two days, and they went out again. "Date tonight with early he paid—he still wants to see me."

Ronnie told me that soon after, in early 1942, Mom showed up at his Blacksburg home and snatched him away from Polly. He was still in the first grade. In her diary the day before, Mom made no mention of Ronnie. She said only that she was heading west by train to see her brother. Boys' Home records show that she removed Ronnie from Polly's the next day. Mom and Ronnie boarded a bus for Covington, where they caught a cab out to the mountainous orphanage.

The home admitted Ronnie at 6:30 p.m. At six years old, he was already four foot four. He weighed sixty pounds. He told me that Mom sat him down on his cot in a cottage, announced that she, not Polly, was his mother, and left him there as she jumped back into the taxi for her long journey home to Keswick. I hate to think she'd treat her own child so coldly, but she must have felt cornered. Here she was poised to finally gain respectability when this boy reappears and threatens it all.

Ronnie remembered it as the worst day of his life. In photos, he went from a carefree, contented-looking boy to an apprehensive waif.

WITH RONNIE TUCKED away, Mom, now twenty-six, went on with her life. She switched her watch to "war time," or daylight saving time. She traveled with Buddy and his family to South Carolina. She read *Gone with the Wind*. She went to movies with Daddy, listened to Guy Lombardo on the radio, and planned her springtime wedding. She received her first wedding gift, a white satin nightie, from Nano. In 450 diary entries over two years, Mom mentioned Ronnie only four times—the first time as "R.," then as "Ronald." How had she gone from "sweetest thing on earth" to barely mentioning him?

She and Daddy married in April 1942, exactly nine months after they met. Mom felt too stained by her unwed pregnancy to buy herself a white dress, so she picked out a blue suit with a little hat topped with silk roses, violets, and gardenias. At the ceremony in a minister's home, Daddy was in a gray suit with black-and-white wing tips. Nano sent a necklace of milky blue moonstones for Mom's trousseau, and later a fat check.

Over the next two weeks, Mom and Daddy hopped from friend to friend and kin to kin on a poor man's honeymoon. The Hicks family in Moneta treated them to lunches and suppers. Nano hosted them in the guest quarters at Hobby Horse. From Daddy's eldest brother's house in Northern Virginia, they visited Washington, D.C., and the Endless Caverns in the Shenandoah Valley of Virginia.

Midway through their honeymoon, they met Polly and drove out to the Covington orphanage with her to see Ronnie. I have one photograph, likely taken by Mom that day. Early is in his wedding suit, rumpled from all the traveling. Mom wanted to show him off to the people at Boys' Home.

My father wears a slight smile as he peers toward the camera. He stands beside Ronnie. The two, not touching, have

their backs to the exterior wall of a building. Ronnie, in light-colored shorts and shirt, squints without smiling at the woman behind the lens. His arms hang close to his sides, his thin legs tight together in a soldier-like stance.

Within days, Adria headed back to work at the McIntyre house. Nano paid for a year's board for Ronnie at Boys' Home. Mom agreed to send a $16.67 money order each month for his incidental needs. Daddy moved back in with his parents. He and Mom didn't have enough money to set up housekeeping together, but soon after, Mom began making payments for a bed big enough for them to share some nights in the maid's quarters.

She used a Zenith Radio Nurse, an early baby monitor, so she could hurry across the house to Buddy's nursery when he cried in the night. When the monitor was in the shop and other times when he was scared or lonely, Buddy slept on the couch in Mom's tiny sitting room.

By the summer of 1942, trouble was brewing again with Polly. She missed Ronnie and regretted letting him go. Two months after Mom and Daddy married, Polly retrieved him for a while from Boys' Home. Once he returned to the orphanage, Polly kept writing to Mom, complaining about the place. I suspect she was also asking why Mom hadn't taken him home with her. After all, Mom had promised that once she married, she and Ronnie would be reunited. Why wasn't that happening?

AT BOYS' HOME, Ronnie harvested corn, milked cows, and did all the farmwork the other boys did. "He had a melancholy look about him," remembered a classmate, who swam

in a creek with Ronnie. "Something used to bother him, but I never knew what. Seemed to be thinking about something more distant."

The orphanage began as an outdoor Sunday school to teach mountain children to read, and it grew into a boarding school for homeless or troubled boys. The boys butchered hogs, canned tomatoes, and produced their own beef, chicken, eggs, fruits, and vegetables.

Polly soon began campaigning to get Ronnie back for good. At first, Mom wrote to the home's superintendent, Dr. E. Reinhold Rogers, that it would be all right with her if Ronnie returned to Polly. She added, however, that she and Daddy hoped to have Ronnie with them soon. "Since my husband's father is going blind, both his father and mother depend on him so we aren't able to have a home of our own yet."

It was then that Ronnie's fate teetered most precariously. Over Ronnie's more than two years at Boys' Home, correspondence between Mom and Rogers revealed their growing alliance against Polly. They chafed at her charges that Mom didn't want him and that the home was neglecting him. They shared the view that Polly had spoiled Ronnie. His housemother reported that he couldn't put on his shoes or wash his face.

The next year, when Ronnie was breaking rules, Rogers pressed Mom to take him as soon as she could: "Perhaps his chief need is for his mother's care . . ." Rogers was pushing Mom's guilt button.

She quickly replied,

I wish it was so I could take him, it would make me happier than anything I could possibly do. As soon as

we can have a home of our own we intend to take him.
My husbands [sic] *mother and father both depend on*
him, and his father is blind—that is why I have to work
and why I can't take Ronald. It would never work out
if Ronald and I tried to live with his [Daddy's] *parents,*
even if he made enough money to care for us all. As you
know a farmer makes very little. I feel like you may
think that I don't want Ronald, but it is the one thing
I look forward to most of all. My husband is very fond
of him too. I hope you see what I mean. I'd never feel
right to leave an old couple with no way of making a
living, and at the same time I want to have Ronald
with me.

Mom moved into the Bishops' tenant house more than
a mile from Bridlespur, but there again, there was no room
for Ronnie. She nursed my grandmother as she lay dying of
cancer. I doubt my grandparents ever knew that their new
daughter-in-law had a son.

Rogers gave Ronnie, then eight, a Stanford-Binet person-
ality and intelligence test and concluded that Ronnie was shy
and inclined to distrust his own abilities. His intelligence
quotient measured somewhat above average at 106.

In the spring of 1944, nearly two years after they married,
Mom and Daddy, the new farm manager, moved into the iso-
lated tenant house where they would spend the next thirty-
seven years.

The farm already felt like home to Daddy. An uncle had
managed the farm for other owners. Daddy earned money for
his first bicycle by thinning peaches there when he was thir-
teen. The tenant house had turned gray as old paint peeled

away. The front porch was rotten in places. But Mom at last had a place for Ronnie.

"Ronald seems to be happy and glad to be home," Mom proudly reported in a letter to Boys' Home after she and Daddy retrieved him.

At first, Ronnie told me, Mom and Daddy were pretty good to him. Being out of the orphanage was a huge relief. But Mom still wasn't claiming him as her son. She told people he was her cousin.

By then she was trying to have Daddy's child. She told me that in her first years with Daddy, she was vigilant with her diaphragm. She didn't want to get pregnant until long after—*really* long after—their wedding. The arithmetic must convince even a simpleton: Yep, no doubt about it, Adria Bishop was married when she conceived. Daddy wanted six children; Mom thought they could only afford one.

Not long after Ronnie arrived and the math was good for her to put her birth control away, Mom suffered a miscarriage. I doubt that Ronnie, then only eight or nine, was aware she'd been pregnant, but Mom was bound to have been gloomy. Daddy wanted her to have his child, and she had failed. She often told me how she was about to flush the fetus down the toilet when Daddy fished it out and buried it in a shoebox in the backyard.

Right after Ronnie's ninth birthday, Mom enrolled him in Cismont School. She was required to submit his Boys' Home records to county school officials. She took the risk that some of them would figure out that Ronnie wasn't really her cousin.

As she sent him off to school that fall, Ronnie told me, she grabbed him by the arm, bent down, and whispered through clenched teeth, "Don't you *ever* call me Mama."

Freaky Little Bastard

In my sundress and Mary Janes, I show off at my
fourth birthday party in 1949 in our yard. Ronnie,
fourteen, towers over us. Behind me, first and
third from the left, are Byrd and Buddy McIntyre.
The other kids lived on a neighboring farm.

I can imagine the intense humanity within our tenant
house in the year before I was born: my just-married
folks, a confused little boy, and my granddaddy, Ed Bishop.
A widower now, he'd moved in too.

Ronnie was crazy about Granddaddy, and I would be later.
He was a handsome old man, smart, of noble bearing. "He
had a heart as big as a bushel basket," Ronnie told me, picking
the perfect metaphor for orchardist Ed, who could snap a twig
off a tree and accurately predict its yield.

The tenant house was rough. The pantry lacked shelves for canned vegetables from their garden. Daddy, busy on the farm, kept putting off building them, until Mom put her foot down: No more sex until you do. Daddy built them that afternoon.

Mom was still babysitting Buddy and his little brother, Byrd, up at the big house during the day, while getting reacquainted with Ronnie in the evenings. Early was learning to be a stepdad while tackling the biggest job of his young life: supervising hundreds of acres for fastidious new owners.

The motoring gentry watched for years as Daddy worked along the dangerously narrow shoulder of the highway at Bridlespur's residential entrance to trim ivy on the brick wall and pick up the trash that marred the ornamental gateway to the big house. One day, he found a bent-up bicycle along the roadside. Granddaddy urged him to repair it and give it to Ronnie, who'd never had a bike.

Daddy told me that he and Mom looked pitiful during their early married years. "*Poor*-poor" is how he described them, and he was not one for exaggeration. Their clothes were shabby. The cook at the big house felt sorry for them. Daddy fixed up the bike and sold it for ten dollars. Ronnie never forgave him. Daddy's desperate need for that ten bucks didn't come across to nine-year-old Ronnie. "They didn't have any feeling for me," he later told me.

During that period, Mom took Ronnie to Moneta to see his grandpa Emmett. They walked up as the old man was using a mechanical device to separate cream from raw milk. The cream wasn't collecting at the top of the separator as it should. Grandpa blamed it on Ronnie's presence. He seemed to think the bastard kid jinxed it, or that's how it seemed to Ronnie.

Another time, on a hot day, Mom left Ronnie and a dog

sweltering in a car while she attended a long service inside her childhood church. She didn't want to have to explain who he was. "She didn't know what to do with me. She couldn't cope," Ronnie later told me. As Ronnie perceived it, when people looked at him, they thought, *You freaky little bastard.* When Daddy's favorite brother visited from out of town, Mom sent Ronnie to his room. Ronnie felt like an outcast.

Mom beat him "hard and often," according to Ronnie. Many times he'd done nothing wrong, but when she was anxious or frustrated, such as when riding in the back seat of that lead-footed brother-in-law's speeding Buick, she'd haul off and whack Ronnie on the head. Somehow the head whacks when she was under pressure felt true to me, even though I hadn't been a victim of them.

SOME YEARS AGO, I drove two hours to the funeral of one of my favorite old ladies from our former church in Keswick. I was at the reception afterward when an elderly woman greeted me from a chair, "Mary Carter Bishop!" Then she said four surprising words: "I taught your brother." I had never before found anyone in Keswick who knew that Ronnie was my brother. Gladys Leake, Ronnie's teacher at Cismont School and an occasional principal by the time I got there, learned from a Moneta friend that Ronnie was Mom's son, not her cousin. Gladys kept that secret for sixty years, until she heard from her friend that I was writing about Ronnie. Soon after that funeral, I went to see Gladys.

"He was one of my very favorite children. He was smart, sweet, clean, neat. I thought he had potential, really, to be great," she told me. But Ronnie had a thick shell around him.

One day, Gladys announced to the class that an attendance officer would be visiting the following morning. The man traveled round the school system giving kids pep talks about concentrating on their studies and not missing school. Ronnie brought a knife in his sock the next day and laid it on his desk. He told Gladys he was afraid the man might take him away.

Gladys presented this to me as a more or less harmless incident, but one of Ronnie's classmates told me later that the knife was about eight inches long and that Ronnie was plunking it menacingly into his wooden desk. Gladys deputized several big boys to wrestle it from Ronnie. Another time, when kids were outside during recess, he went back inside and turned all the desks upside down.

Gladys tried repeatedly to break through Ronnie's walls. "I said, 'You should open up and talk about your problems with people.' He said, 'But she . . . ,' and then he must have thought, 'I won't say any more.' He never said a word about your mother. Just the 'but she.' He's been on my mind all these years. I loved him dearly. I still love him. But he was someone I couldn't help."

ANY ATTENTION RONNIE got from Mom and Daddy shrank immediately upon my birth in 1945. From that day forward, Ronnie moved to the permanent back burner in the Bishop household.

At last, Adria was a legitimate, seal-of-approval mother. That she named me Mary signaled her hope that I'd be pure and saintly. Her community cheered my birth. Anne McIntyre's mother, Julia Sophie du Pont Andrews, sent a sterling silver baby cup engraved with my name and birth date. Nano

McIntyre sent a decorated white flannel Christmas stocking from FAO Schwarz in New York. Mom's Roanoke friend and landlady Mallie Moran sent a tiny brush and comb, and a pink silk jacket.

When I was ten months old, Mom took a picture of Ronnie and me in the side yard at our house. I'm standing in my diaper and a light-colored dress inside a wooden playpen that was elevated—raised, I suppose, so chickens, dogs, cats, and snakes couldn't reach me while Mom did her housework. Rolling hills and the Southwest Mountains stretch behind us. Thin, long-limbed Ronnie, ten years old, wearing a plaid shirt, shorts, and a faint smile, stands beside the pen with his left hand supporting my back.

When I was about four and Ronnie around fourteen, Mom ordered him to take off all his clothes and stand naked in our tiny front foyer. Ronnie's head dropped forward and his eyes were cast down as Mom dusted him head to toe with what I remember being an asthma powder, but it could have been a pesticide because by that time he was sleeping in the barn. She delivered it with a pump-action duster that she worked vigorously, as if she were killing those tobacco worms back in Moneta. Her eyes blinked rapidly and her face was angry, as if she didn't want to see Ronnie's skeletal frame. He looked as humiliated as any kid I'd ever seen. It was my first glimpse of Mom as another kind of mother.

Except for that memory and other general recollections of him as a gloomy, unwelcome presence at our house, my memory bank of Ronnie as a boy is empty. It was only through my conversations with him, decades later, that I filled in the blanks.

When Mom and Daddy took us anywhere in the farm

pickup, I, the little princess, rode up front with them. Ronnie rode in back. He said I was a mean little shit to him. Deep in my mind is a filmy recollection of sticking my tongue out at him. He had to have been jealous and resentful, and how he acted that out toward me, I don't know. I still sleep with my hands protecting my throat, and for no reason I know, I imagine that somebody's peering in the window at me. I fear waking up to find an intruder by my bed. Ronnie told me that he spied on other people in Keswick. Why wouldn't he have spied on my cozy life as a child basking in the adoration he'd once had from Polly and Roy?

Daddy told me that Ronnie's and Mom's personalities clashed and that Ronnie was rebellious. My folks were stumped as to what to do. When he was twelve and I was two, they enrolled him at Miller School, then a private boarding school for poor white boys in the Blue Ridge Mountains twenty-five miles from Keswick. It was a cross between an orphanage and a reformatory. For Ronnie, it was Boys' Home all over again—mandatory farm labor, rigorous academics, vocational training, this time with a more military regimen. In an undated photo taken by our front porch, Ronnie wears a grayish-blue wool cadet-style uniform with black stripes running down the sides of his pants and on his jacket.

At the annual Miller School reunion in June 2015, I learned that Ronnie's nickname was Slim Idaho. Classmates couldn't remember why the "Idaho." (Did Ronnie like potatoes?) But Ronnie called himself Slim for the rest of his life. Right before their picnic that day, in the shadow of the brick buildings where Ronnie labored and studied, the sweet old alums of Miller School christened me Sister Slim.

Except for two pairs of bibbed overalls issued each year,

the boys produced their own necessities. They even bent the rails of their iron bed frames over the anvils in the school's forge. On the school's fifteen-hundred-acre farm, they milked the cows, picked the lima beans, shucked the corn, baked the bread.

Ronnie and the other boys slept in the unheated top-floor dormitories of Old Main, the Victorian building that's still the heart of the school. When it snowed, the boys were forced to clamber out the windows to the high roof and sweep it clean to prevent leaks when it melted. The alums said the roof was slick, and it's a wonder none of them fell off. As temperatures dipped, the school issued each boy three blankets—one in October, one in November, one in December. A glass of water left in the dorm froze overnight.

Each boy's first year, he was declared a New Boy and forced to submit to the wishes of all who'd been there longer, the Old Boys. Ronnie shined their shoes, brought them water, and absorbed without lip the punches to his arms that any Old Boy might throw in a hallway. If he whined, they'd punch again, harder.

I asked Ronnie's classmates how he reacted to this *Lord of the Flies* hierarchy. How aggressively did he lord it over the next wave of New Boys when he had his chance during his second year? They didn't recall, yet one of them did offer this: "If I remember right, he kept to himself. Some guys just didn't fit in."

At first, Ronnie bought into Miller School's promise that if he behaved himself, he'd be rewarded with a decent job after graduation. Less cooperative boys warned him that the school was a crock. "They were right," Ronnie told me. "It turned them into professional shoeshine boys." Actually, quite a few of

his classmates became school principals, career military men, construction contractors, and well-respected businessmen.

In the spring of 1949, the school's superintendent expelled thirteen-year-old Ronnie, then in the eighth grade. The record says only that Ronnie had shown a "disregard for rules." Alums said that the superintendent was stern. They remembered the rubber paddle he flayed on their rear ends and the patterns its cut-out holes left in their hides.

Ronnie came back home to Bridlespur that spring but rarely approached our house, mostly sleeping in the barn. He went to work as a bag boy at the A&P grocery in Charlottesville, then as a caddy at Farmington Country Club in town. He set up an account at Morris' Store at Keswick, where he bought potted meat, Vienna sausages, saltines, and when golf tips were good, strawberry ripple ice cream.

Ronnie insisted to me that our mother didn't want him at our house and that she denied him food. I don't know the truth about that, but I have no recollection of him eating with us or sleeping in the house, although he must have slept inside before I was born and when I was too young to remember. After his stint in the barn, early in his teens, he and friends from nearby farms, including preteen Buddy McIntyre, built a two-story log cabin up on the mountain for him to sleep in.

Daddy helped with construction of the pine-log hut. He contributed long barked slabs from trees he milled for fence boards, and he joined the young guys in nailing the steep roof together. The cabin was only eight by ten feet but tall enough that Ronnie, already six feet of his eventual six foot four, could stand up straight even on the second floor. With its steep roof, it looked more like a chapel than a house.

The cabin sat near the property line between Bridlespur

and the nineteenth-century estate next door, Ben Coolyn, Scottish for "breezy mountain." Charlie Hallock and his family moved into Ben Coolyn's manor house on Charlie's eleventh birthday in 1950. Ronnie, then fourteen, was a wonder to Charlie and his three brothers. He was the rare kid who answered to no adult. Charlie didn't learn until years later who Ronnie really was.

A free agent, irreverent, Ronnie came and went as he pleased. He provided the Hallock boys with their first cigarettes and soft-core porn called blue books—pulp magazines featuring racy pictures, stories of derring-do, and science fiction.

Ronnie roamed Keswick like an undercover agent. He crept around the houses and peered in at the rich people in their dining rooms and in their bedrooms. For all its high-class charm, Keswick, to Ronnie, was a vulgar, craven place.

With all his prowling and peering, he was tweaking the monster's tail. Keswick's servant class customarily looked the other way at wild behavior by the rich, but here was Ronnie trespassing on Keswick's most precious commodity: the freedom of the elite to do as they pleased, safe from prying eyes.

Ronnie had been stealing food from the estates for years. From his mountain refuge, he could wander an array of bountiful farms from their unprotected back acres. They were his buffet. He sampled fresh food from gardens, orchards, meat houses, and kitchens. With pride, Ronnie bragged to me how he pilfered figs, grapes, and peaches. He itemized, with the gusto of a gourmand, his early scores as a hungry boy: a head of cabbage, a jar of homegrown fruit, a pint of preserves, and cartons of frozen peaches. He broke into smokehouses, sliced meat off the hanging hams, and cooked it over an open fire.

The kitchen at Ben Coolyn was Ronnie's greatest temptation. The Hallock boys occasionally spirited him into their house against the wishes of their parents. Ronnie knew that the boys' mother kept her pantry fully stocked for her sons. In the middle of the night, Ronnie would unscrew the window screen in the Hallocks' kitchen and climb inside. His most cherished booty was two angel food cakes. He'd fumble around in the darkness for canned goods. Often he'd get back to his campfire and curse his rotten luck that he'd bagged only cans of tomato paste, unpalatable even to a starving boy. The Hallocks came to expect Ronnie's food burglaries, one of them told me. "Something would be missing, and we'd say, 'That was probably Ronnie.'"

By the early fifties, when I was an oblivious first grader and Ronnie was sixteen, he was ramping up his thievery. Ronnie admitted to me later that he stole a sword, a gun, and a woman's purse containing forty dollars.

On the other side of Ben Coolyn, middle-aged Leon Sebring Dure Jr. had moved into East Belmont Farm, an expansive estate with a Federal-style house built early in the nineteenth century. Dure, former White House correspondent for the *Washington Post* and managing editor of the *Richmond Times-Dispatch*, would soon become a key player in Virginia white leaders' search for a way around court-mandated school desegregation. Dure invented "freedom of choice" as a way to keep most schools racially exclusive. Under his plan, white families received state grants for their children to attend all-white private schools. His system was struck down by federal courts in the late sixties.

When Ronnie filched weapons from East Belmont, he

would learn for himself that Leon Dure was not a man to be
toyed with. Ronnie hid one of Dure's .22 rifles in a hay bale
on another farm. A farmer discovered it when he went to feed
his cows. I remember Mr. Dure—all rich people were "Mr."
or "Mrs." to us—and he was an austere, formidable figure. He
and the other powerful men and women of Keswick began to
compare their notes on Ronnie Overstreet. They'd all been
had by this renegade boy. They vowed to rein him in, and
Mom and Daddy were targets too.

IN THE FALL of 1952, Leon Dure and his wife convened a
summit of Keswick landowners fed up with Ronnie's intru-
sions. They called in county sheriff's deputies and summoned
Mom to the library at the McIntyres' house, where *New
Yorker* magazines lay askew on the coffee table and horse
show ribbons adorned the pine-paneled walls. Buddy McIn-
tyre Sr. sat behind his desk. The Dures and other neighbors
sat on the oxblood leather sofa and chairs.

Before Ronnie's nocturnal prowling, these estate owners
had never felt the need to lock their doors. Now, for the first
time, they were locking them, and they didn't like it. They
told Mom that she'd better do something about Ronnie,
or else. She took it to mean that she, Daddy, Ronnie, and I
would be kicked off the farm. For Daddy to lose his job and
our home would throw us into peril just as we were getting
established—and it all would be because Mom gave birth to
that illegitimate kid way back when. Years later, she would re-
member her humiliation that day. "Those old buzzards," she
said of the men, and perhaps women too, who called her on

the carpet. Left to choose between her first child and her new family—Daddy and me—she chose us. In some sense, she had already chosen by leaving Ronnie to fend for himself.

I don't know where I was when she faced that day's ultimatum. For decades I had no clue what went down. I was seven years old. It was a Saturday. My folks must have given me strict orders to stay in the house, or else they sent me to somebody else's house, which was a rarity.

I don't know if my parents tricked Ronnie into being captured, but if they did, he would have smelled a rat. At least three deputies were present. Knowing what I do now about Ronnie's lifelong defiance of authority figures, I doubt he calmly turned himself in. I imagine that his long legs carried him across the fields and into the woods, and when they caught him, that he fought like a wildcat.

He was seventeen years old, already six foot two, and underweight at 128 pounds. Ronnie told me he was jammed between two deputies in the back of a squad car as they roared out of Bridlespur's farm road, headed for the highway. Destination: Western State Hospital, a notorious mental institution in Staunton, forty miles west of Charlottesville.

I DON'T KNOW who suggested Ronnie go there. Mom and Daddy, they both told me later, believed a mental hospital was a better place for him than a home for delinquents, where Ronnie would fall in with other bad boys. They weren't sure what to do. But they were certain about one thing: They had to obey the farm owners' orders to stop his stealing.

Since opening as the Western State Lunatic Asylum in 1828, the sprawling hospital was known throughout Virginia as a

dismal, punishing place. Whenever I or any of my kid friends acted up, our mothers were sure to warn, "You'd better watch out or they'll send you to Staunton." Ronnie must have heard it too. Just like me, he never thought it would actually happen.

For most of the first half of the twentieth century, Western State was run by Dr. Joseph DeJarnette, one of the nation's most maniacal eugenicists. In 1947, when he retired at age eighty, he was still urging Virginia to quadruple its sterilizations of sick, poor, and socially disfavored people. He himself claimed to have personally sterilized six hundred men.

Ronnie assured me that he wasn't sterilized at Western State, and his name does not appear on the Virginia Hospital Board's list of individuals compelled to be sterilized during the period he was there.

In 2009, I filed a request for Ronnie's records at Western State. It had been so long since he was there and that institution had changed so much, I doubted those records still existed. A few weeks later, I found a large envelope in my mailbox, return address: Western State Hospital. I took it to a quiet place in my house and opened it. Inside I found twenty-six heartbreaking pages that brought to life the drama that was playing out at home when I was too young to understand.

It was October 4, 1952, when the deputies brought Ronnie to Western State. Documents completed during his first days there threw many preliminary diagnoses at him. They stated that he was mentally ill—and mentally retarded—and that he suffered from delusions of persecution. A doctor examined him at five thirty that evening. Ronnie had a watch and thirty-five cents in his pocket. A social worker summed up his recent history: "Home environment good. Resents being

corrected by mother. Threatens to injure mother by force.
Patient wanders, threatens others and steals guns."

The most disturbing pages for me were that social worker's
notes from October 22, 1952, eighteen days after Ronnie's ar-
rival, when my parents went in for a visit—I must have been
left with friends of theirs. The pain of all the parties, even my
own, is vivid. It was difficult to read my mother's self-serving
account of Ronnie's behavior.

> Patient's mother and step-father came to the office
> today as requested for a history interview. Mrs. Bishop
> was a large, young appearing woman, neatly but
> cheaply dressed. She and Mr. Bishop seemed about
> the same age. They were pleasant and cooperative,
> answered questions readily and gave some spontaneous
> information. Mrs. Bishop expressed a desire to help
> the patient in any way she could, but showed little real
> warmth when speaking of him. Her husband came to
> the patient's defense several times with the remark that
> several accusations had not been proven against the boy.

Mom, then thirty-six, told the social worker that from
early childhood on, Ronnie had a "very high temper." She
noted also that he'd had an asthma attack the night before he
was picked up on the farm and brought to the hospital. The
social worker continued:

> His half sister, age seven, seemed to like him although
> he would frighten her at times. He has for the last year
> threatened his mother, called her names, drawn pictures
> in which he would be shooting or stabbing her. He stole

various articles in the community—axes, guns, knives and liquor, and the sheriff warned them that something would have to be done. Informants refused to permit him to bring stolen articles into the house, so he hid them in a cabin he and some boys built in the woods. He frequently wore a long dagger in his belt.

Recently Mrs. Bishop has been very much afraid of the patient. He has threatened her many times, but has not actually tried to hurt her physically. However, informants had no control over him. He stayed out the better part of the night. Often, when he came in in the early morning hours, his eyes would look "glassey" [sic] and his mother believes he was either drinking or taking dope. She has seen him drink on only one occasion, but empty whiskey bottles have been found in his room.

As far as it is known, patient has never actually had a date. Last year he went to a neighbor's house nearly every night, possibly to see the neighbor's daughter. The daughter was about 25 years old. The neighbor asked patient not to come so often, since the daughter had other boy friends. Shortly after this, patient let all of the air out of the neighbor's tires and it is reported that he damaged other property around her home. He reads a number of "sexy" magazines.

Patient is very particular to keep his face and hands clean, to wear a clean shirt, shine his shoes and comb his hair. However, he refused to take a bath and seldom has his hair cut.

In a separate interview, Ronnie had his say. He asserted that Mom and Daddy had rejected him and made him feel

unwanted. They gave all their attention to me and wouldn't even help him with schoolwork. They treated him like a baby. Though Ronnie admitted to me later that he stole at least one gun, he denied it when questioned at the hospital. He acknowledged that he had few friends. "There's just a bunch of rich boys at Keswick where I live. I've always stayed more or less to myself."

During a mental test, when Ronnie failed to name four types of fish, his interviewer wrote that he exploded: "Jesus Christ, much as I fish and I can't think of the names of them."

A psychologist observed marked feelings of inferiority in Ronnie, who made a reference to "someone dumb like me." She found his references to rich Keswick boys "wistful" and noted that his ambition was to attend night school and to get an "important" office job. She found his responses to her questions normal, although she said, "Anxiety and anger, sometimes well concealed, seemed to be the predominant reactions." She came to the conclusion that he was of normal intelligence.

Three weeks after his arrival, Western State began administering electroshock treatments to Ronnie. I still don't know why. In all, he would undergo at least five of them in less than a month. Because Ronnie was still a minor, I assume Mom gave her consent, although no such permission was mentioned in his records.

In notes from a psychotherapy session after the treatments, Ronnie argued insightfully that electroshock was hardly likely to help: "They can keep me here for fifty years or shock me one thousand times and I'll still have the problem to solve when I get home." Presumably, he meant the friction between him and his mother.

Earlier that month, he'd appeared for an interview before a roomful of hospital officials, including six physicians and three psychologists. Ronnie told them he came to Western State because of disagreements with his parents:

> *I didn't get along with them too well, and things were going from bad to worse. I went out one night and came in about midnight and was accused of stealing some things. Two of the charges got proved against me. Things seemed to just get worse and worse, and they finally decided to put me in this place.*
>
> *I have a sister who is 7 years old; that's another thing. She is actually their child, and I guess that made them want to do more for her than they did for me. I just got fed up with that, got to running around, and got into trouble. I never took any dope of any kind in my life. I have drunk some—just a little.*

Throughout the records, Ronnie refers variously to Mom as his cousin, his aunt, his grandmother, and his guardian. He said she wasn't his "real" mother. Ronnie admitted that he'd threatened to kill her, "but she knew I didn't mean it. It was about the only thing I could think of to keep her from picking on me. If you let me out to go back home, I'll prove to you that I wouldn't hurt her."

Toward the end of the interview, Ronnie said he thought our mother would be glad if he left home forever, but "at my age and with no high school education, I couldn't make a go of it, I don't think."

In a transcript of the post-interview discussion, panel members disagreed on whether Ronnie was psychotic, borderline

psychotic, or understandably distraught over the way his life had panned out. Some considered him dangerously hostile. Another, a Polish-born psychiatrist new to the hospital, offered this opinion: "I don't think he's psychotic, but just reacting to everything like a boy would do. He's just an unhappy boy who has had a difficult life."

The psychologist who wrote the main reports on Ronnie's mental condition thought Ronnie was "just a little psychotic, and maybe still salvageable." They finally compromised by calling his condition a "schizophrenic reaction," unspecified, with a passive-aggressive personality. They noted Ronnie's extreme stress—"rejection by mother; poor home situation."

Ronnie didn't tell me much about Western State—only that there were no other kids in his building, just a bunch of loony grown-ups. To pass the time, he washed staff members' cars. They told him he had no business being there. A psychologist there lectured Mom on her role in Ronnie's behavior, which incensed her. Forever after, she had a low regard for mental health workers of all kinds.

Four months after Ronnie's admission, the hospital bosses sent him to a barber school at nearby Woodrow Wilson Rehabilitation Center, a state-run center that Ronnie recalled also trained disabled and wayward citizens in welding, clock and watch repair, and other employable trades. "Three square meals and they didn't shock you"—a welcome change for Ronnie.

When his Western State psychotherapist called him in for a final assessment, Ronnie told him that he was contented at barber school and that he was going to dances and picnics on the weekends. "When I think of the way I behaved for a while there, I blush. I thought everybody was against me; that

everybody was my enemy and I had to get them before they got me. I sure was mixed up." To me, this sounds like Ronnie spoon-feeding the big dogs what they wanted to hear, but hey, whatever worked.

I don't know if Mom and Daddy visited Ronnie. Hospital notes make no mention of it.

I don't remember ever seeing him at Western State. I was there only once, as far as I recall, and it was disturbing. It was my college psychology class field trip, in the sixties. All I remember is crazed men with grimaced faces, their tongues wagging out, leering and raving from behind caged windows as I and my female classmates minced nervously into the auditorium for a show-and-tell about mental illness. When I saw the movie *One Flew Over the Cuckoo's Nest* in 1975, it reminded me of Western State with all its mad people warehoused in forbidding old buildings and dragged off to shock treatments. I had no idea my own brother had been one of them.

I asked two senior mental health professionals—a clinical psychologist and a psychiatrist—to read Ronnie's records. Neither saw the slightest indication that Ronnie was schizophrenic. The extensive hospital notes mention no visions, voices, or hallucinations, which are typical with schizophrenia. Both clinicians said the productive track of Ronnie's life, which began the moment he was released and continued unabated until his death thirty-eight years later, disproved the diagnosis.

When Ronnie first arrived at the hospital, staffers thought he had delusions of persecution. But was he imagining that his mother had cast him aside? Was he imagining that he was an embarrassment to her? Ronnie was angry with Mom, and

how, really, could he not have been? She rejected him. She tore him away from Polly and Roy and sent him to an orphanage, then a reform school, then a mental hospital.

As terrifying as Ronnie's electroshock treatments must have been, he was lucky he didn't have a lobotomy while at Western State, as did many patients during that time.

The last item in Ronnie's file is a letter from Mom to hospital administrators early in 1954. She wanted them to know that late the preceding August, after ten months in state custody, Ronnie went to work at the American Barber Shop in downtown Roanoke. "As far as I know," she wrote, "he is doing all right."

Truth at the Kitchen Stove

Photos found among Ronnie's possessions after
his death show the change in his spirits from his
happy, bountiful years with Polly and Roy to, a
few years later, his untrusting gaze as he stood a
few miles from the orphanage where our mother
sent him in 1942.

Over the next many years, with Ronnie gone, my folks
made a long, hard climb, me in tow, to a fingertip's
touch on the lowest rung of the middle class. Ronnie ben-
efited not one iota. I don't remember asking where he'd
gone.

He was right about Granddaddy Bishop being a grand old
man. He entertained me with his merry ice-blue eyes and that
thick silver mustache I tugged on, making him yowl in comic
pain. Eventually, he moved out of our house and into town

for the most implausible of jobs for an old blind man—that of night watchman.

Every month or two, Mom, Daddy, and I rode the pickup to Moneta to see my other grandpa and Miss Belle, now in a farmhouse Belle's better-off sister rented for them. All I recall is a rickety back porch, a corncrib, the purr of contented chickens pecking at the ground, a lonely clock ticking in the sparsely furnished parlor, and more love than they ever offered Ronnie.

Moneta was a revelation to Daddy and to me. All we'd ever known were rich landowners and poor grunts like Daddy who wrestled vast geographies into idyllic showplaces. In Moneta, small farmers fed themselves out of their own rugged slices of earth. They prayed for more rain or less rain, and other than that, answered to no one.

My folks made the most of our dependent circumstances. They painted our tenant house white. Daddy refloored and screened the front porch. They planted lilacs, maples, mimosas, and an elm, creating a lush oasis in the middle of pastureland. Mom culled impatiens seeds from friends' yards, and within a few years her flowers shimmered in a thigh-high bank of purple, pink, and red in the shadow of our porch. We put tables out there, and as lightning bugs blinked across the fields, our church friends dined on Mom's just-decapitated-on-the-stump fried chicken, and biscuits made with hand-churned buttermilk. They nibbled cobs of Daddy's hybrid yellow-and-white corn, which he called "cream and sugar." Mom made peach ice cream and spiked her sweet iced tea with mint snipped from our creek out back.

Except for hungry black men asking permission to hunt groundhogs on the farm, we had hundreds of acres to ourselves most days after Daddy's farm crew went home. Nothing lay

between us and the mountains. No power lines, no buildings, nothing but wind, weather, and natural spectacle playing across the bumble-buzzed fields.

When I was nine, we watched from our front porch as Hurricane Hazel bent, but did not break, the giant trees a pasture away that made possible Mommy's trademark brown-sugar pecan cookies. Another night we stepped into our front yard for a rare Southern aurora borealis that billowed pink and green curtains of light above the Southwest Mountains.

When I was little, Mom and Daddy began a practice that would later make my knocking on strangers' doors as a reporter feel like old times. She delivered slices of pound cake or pecan cookies whenever she heard people were sick, lonely, or grieving. I tagged along to worn plantation cabins where kitchen doorways were so low even I at an early age ducked my head. At one house, a couple's three drooling, moaning teenaged sons' muscular dystrophy had turned their living room into a field hospital. The boys flopped their long limbs wildly on their beds as their feet contracted from muscle spasms, and I felt lucky.

We'd started attending South Plains Presbyterian Church, a 130-year-old congregation up the road from Bridlespur. A one-room church with clear blown-glass windows and a plain interior, South Plains steeped my folks in a rigid, hardworking Calvinism—key to Mom's plan to make us respectable. She and Daddy gave up liquor and didn't drink again until I was out of college. (At least four of Daddy's six brothers and sisters were alcoholics. Mom's drunken brother died when he fell, or was conked on the head, outside his favorite Ohio bar; the ninety dollars he'd flaunted was missing from his shirt pocket.)

South Plains was a cozy little white working-class congregation, where sun-scorched farmhands bowed their lily-white foreheads in their only hatless waking hour of the week. Every Sunday morning, Mom ironed Daddy's shirt and parted his hair, which she'd shampooed the night before as he soaked off the farm dirt in our cast-iron tub. Daddy became the church's top elected layman.

Mom was recruited for top roles, but she declined. She didn't tell them why, but it was Ronnie. "I wasn't worthy. I sinned," she explained later. Still, she'd slip into her brown-and-white spectator pumps to lead the church women and the local home economics club. In the years following Ronnie's departure, she was finally recovering from the taint of having had him.

Daddy was mentored by our minister, a progressive, pipe-puffing intellectual of Scottish descent, the fifth generation in his family to minister to humble farmers. The two men leaned on Bridlespur's fences for hours to talk about nature, God, and agriculture. I was mentored by his wife, Fanny, a college-trained biologist who showed me the design of spiderwebs and the life cycle of *Lunaria annua*, the money plant, with seedpods like silver dollars. She introduced me to *National Geographic*, cranked up her Metropolitan Opera records, and encouraged my folks to think about piano lessons and college for me. Before my teens, I was banging out an off-tune "Come Thou Fount of Every Blessing" on the church's tinny upright.

Fanny was the first woman I knew who shunned permanents, girdles, and stockings. Ladylike, with her bare knees together and her skirt tucked around them, her shiny brown hair carefully pinned into a bun, she was lovely without makeup. I'd sit by her in church and watch as she observed birds through the windows during her husband's long prayers.

The women of South Plains found her odd. They whispered as she slipped their home-baked ham biscuits into her purse at potlucks so she wouldn't have to cook that night. Farm wives took pride in fattening their husbands; a man's beefy frame advertised his wife's good cooking. Fanny was so thrifty that she'd cut a slice of Wonder Bread in two—the long way—for a sandwich so thin the tomato showed pink through the bread. Her husband was skinny. Visiting a friend's bathroom, she once sprinkled powder into her shoes, only to discover, as the skin of her soles began to pucker, that it wasn't talcum; it was dental adhesive.

I wanted to be like Fanny—my own authentic, quirky self, not so concerned with what people thought. This plan didn't align with Mom's for me.

She and I would wrestle for the next sixty years over the tension represented by the church ladies and Fanny—between behaving conventionally and feeling free to be our own true selves. Mom needed people, especially other women, to approve of her, and as part of that, she needed me to be a docile yes-ma'am kind of girl. I strained at that leash. I was Exhibit A of her attentive mothering. She was forever straightening my collar and fussing with my hair. Couldn't she see that all that self-consciousness was no way to live?

CHRISTMAS MORNINGS, WE'D put on our Sunday best and ride the pickup over to the McIntyres' to admire their tree and sip eggnog from silver cups. They might give us a jar of kumquats from their new winter place in Florida, or in the heyday of John F. Kennedy, an authentic Massachusetts rocker like his. Later on, they shocked us with the gift of a hundred

shares of General Motors stock, millions of which, because of an antitrust controversy, were being divested by du Pont descendants like Anne McIntyre.

Mom was trying to squelch her self-doubts, but she never learned to drive. She practiced in the stick-shift pickup on the farm road until she crashed through a gate. A dog leapt out the back and ran away. Daddy and I teased her: Even the dog's scared of your driving. She quit. We robbed her of self-respect. Driving would have done wonders for her confidence.

She took charge anyway. There wouldn't be enough money from Daddy's check for my college tuition, so when I was eleven, she signed on as a department store clerk. Another downtown worker out our way drove her for a dollar a week. The cook at the big house who'd felt sorry for us because of our worn clothes cheered the new outfits bought with Mom's store discount.

I'd linger along the aisles of the high-ceilinged main floor, inhale cologne spritzes wafting from the perfume counter, take in the pleasant chatter of women shoppers talking with the clerks, and savor this twinkly scene of midcentury commerce. Mom was doing so much better that she urged other Keswick women and their daughters to work there, giving them all a leg up.

After ten years, though, Mom was fed up with the low pay. She saw old women working there on wobbly legs because their meager Social Security wouldn't allow them to retire. Mom became a medical records clerk at the University of Virginia School of Medicine, with health insurance, a pension plan, and a credit union. At lunch break on her first payday, she rode the bus all the way back to the store to show her friends her pay stub.

Because of Mom, I went to college—the first in her family—and because I went to college, I went to graduate school and earned two master's degrees. Because of her, she and Daddy traveled to Canada, the Great Lakes, and New England, and because of her, they eventually bought their first home, paying it off in an astonishing six months.

IN THE MIDDLE of June 1978, I came home to Bridlespur. I was getting ready to wander around Europe for five months, something I don't think even the McIntyres had done.

For all my misgivings about Keswick, once I moved to noisier, dirtier places like Washington, New York, and Philadelphia, I came to appreciate the place. I would return and collapse like everybody else into the peace of its calming hills.

I was at the top of my game. I was thirty-two and divorced, having saved myself from an unhappy marriage. I was an up-and-coming investigative reporter in the heady era after Woodward and Bernstein drove Richard Nixon from the White House. I'd earned a master's degree from Columbia University's Graduate School of Journalism and gone to work for the *Charlotte Observer* in North Carolina, a paper dedicated to fearless journalism. Now the *Philadelphia Inquirer*, the *Observer*'s big sister in the Knight-Ridder newspaper chain, wanted to hire me.

Newspapers had pushed through my shyness. Either I got out there and interviewed people, or I'd wind up in a secretarial pool. Before long, I liked nothing more than rapping on doors on backstreets and country roads, taking in the wringer washers on porches, the long johns on the clothesline, the linoleum

worn to wood in front of the kitchen sink from a lifetime of dishwashing.

For the *Observer*, I'd written a biographical series on Charlotte's favorite son, evangelist Billy Graham, and it was about to be made into a quickie hardback by a New York publisher. For a week's worth of rewrites, they'd paid me $10,000, more than enough for Europe.

I ARRIVED AT Bridlespur late one evening, my Volkswagen Beetle stuffed with clothes to sort through for my trip. I hugged and kissed my folks, dropped my luggage at the bottom of the narrow stairs, and hurried up to my old room to bed.

Sleep at our house was limb-stretching bliss. Our two upstairs bedrooms, my folks' and mine, shared a common chimney that pierced the middle of the century-old house. Each spring, Daddy installed fans in the fireplace of each bedroom. We opened windows at the heads of our beds, set the fans on reverse, and slept all summer with cool mountain air flowing across our mattresses while the day's heat flew up the chimney. I'd wake up to the songs of meadowlarks and red-winged blackbirds, descendants of the grassland nesters that scored my childhood's soundtrack.

Over the next few days, I bragged to the folks that I would wander around whatever countries I spontaneously chose, and I would do this all alone. That I had the cash, the freedom, the guts, and especially the sense of worth to make this trip amazed them. They savored my supper-table bravado with tickled glances at each other, a wordless celebration: They'd helped their only child position herself to cross the Atlantic for no other reason than her own curiosity.

One reason I was there was that I needed a passport. It would take days for my application to clear, and what sweeter place to wait? I'd lost my birth certificate, a primary requirement for a passport, and Mom didn't have a copy. So one pleasant Wednesday morning I headed out in my navy-blue Bug for an hour's drive to Richmond and the state health department's Bureau of Vital Statistics. The clerk took little time in making a certified copy for me.

I don't remember when it was that I took a good look at the yellow, black, and blue document—maybe as soon as I got in my car, maybe during a gas station stop on the way home to Keswick. I recognized Mom's careful longhand on the certificate. In 1945, when I was born, Virginia's birth certificate was essentially a questionnaire filled out by the mother: the father's name, race, birthplace, occupation, age at the time of the baby's birth, and all the same information for the mother. Daddy was twenty-seven; Mom was twenty-nine. She wrote my name—Mary Carter Bishop—centered on a line and stretched out in a proud, confident script, like, *ta-da*, she was introducing me to the world.

Then I reached section 21, headed "Children Born to This Mother." The question was "How many other children of this mother are now living?" After this, my mother wrote a clear, unequivocal numeral "1."

That was odd. She'd had that miscarriage a year or two before I was born. But how could my extremely cautious mother confuse a long-buried fetus with a living child? She handled bureaucracy with dead seriousness. She wouldn't have slipped up on her only child's birth certificate.

I GOT HOME around five thirty. Mom was frying chicken at the electric stove. "How'd it go?" she asked.

"Good." I watched as she flipped the legs and the thighs. Through the window beside her, tall field grasses moved in the wind.

I needed to know about that birth certificate. I fished it out of my purse in another room and brought it to her. I expected this question to be resolved in a few seconds.

"How come you put a one here?" I pointed to the section on other children. She wiped her hand on her apron and looked at the certificate before handing it back. She didn't raise her voice or look startled when, while turning over a sizzling thigh, she nonchalantly said, "You know who that is."

I stared at her, my face searching hers. "No, I don't know who that is." She laughed stiffly and looked back at the frying pan. How could she think I knew?

Then, with a hint of "you must know" impatience, she uttered two words that sent my worldview reeling:

It's Ronnie.

She dispensed this information as lightly as the flour she was now sprinkling into the pan to make the gravy.

Ronnie Overstreet? That skinny, unhappy kid who lived on the farm when I was little? The boy she said was my cousin?

She told me at the stove that she'd gotten pregnant at eighteen, years before she met Daddy. "I made a mistake," she said, lowering her voice.

Over the next day or so, she revealed that before they married, she told Daddy about Ronnie. Daddy promised never to mention her first pregnancy again, she said, with tears in her eyes, and he never did. To Mom, his silence on the subject was a badge of love.

Daddy came into the kitchen from late-day chores. She whispered something to him. Head-to-head, they shared a private, muted, uncomfortable laugh. The secret they'd kept for decades was out of the cupboard and flitting among us like a moth.

We didn't talk about it at supper. I'd stepped in something sticky. I wanted to scrape it off.

IN THE WAY we often underreact to the biggest news in our lives, I absorbed all this in silence. I wandered away from my folks. I went to my room and fiddled with clothes for my trip.

My God. Ronnie Overstreet was my brother. My *half* brother. But still, my brother.

He was the gloomiest person I'd ever seen. When I was just venturing from my playpen, he was a hunch-shouldered, greasy-haired, asthmatic boy of twelve. He wore rough dark-plaid jackets and hunting caps with the earflaps down, a melancholy boy hidden in sad clothes.

On the rare occasion he was in our house, he quietly glared at us, fuming at our cozy life. In my contentment, I never bothered to wonder where he slept, who fed him, or who took care of him. It was clear my parents were uncomfortable with him around.

This woman, this mother of mine, I didn't know her after all.

Of all the mothers in the world, how could this all-giving one of mine, this overprotective, selfless parent who on so little money dressed me like a little empress, scraped together dollars to rent my high school band clarinet, and packed me off to summer camp, also be the mother of that miserable boy?

THAT NIGHT, I lay in the bed where I'd slept as a child. Of the two upstairs rooms, I had the better one. Daddy needed to be able to look out over the dairy barn, the stables, the cows, the sheep, and to listen for the burglar alarm at the big house. He and Mom took the room on that side.

From my bed I could lie on my stomach and gaze through the window at the head of my bed, across the fields to Sugarloaf Mountain in the distance. In winter, I'd fall asleep in the most delicious of circumstances—snug under quilts and watching snow silently creep over the ridge, knowing I would awake to hear the Motorola radio atop the fridge downstairs announcing there'd be no school.

But that June night when my brother was born in my mind, I lay sleepless in the cool darkness, wondering about Ronnie, who his father was, and how it could be that I had a brother out there somewhere. Even then, I knew Ronnie had it hard; even then, I knew the contrasts between us. The very day I'd felt so cheeky, I'd been pulled back into the family shame.

FINDING AND

LOSING RONNIE

I Walk into His Barbershop

Ronnie in January 1961 when he was twenty-five.

I'd been at the *Philadelphia Inquirer* less than three months when a reactor at central Pennsylvania's Three Mile Island nuclear power plant partly melted, threatening to irradiate an entire region. Residents fleeing the area in cars packed with kids and dogs looked quizzical as I and an army of other reporters rushed by them toward the scene. I played only a small part in the 1979 coverage but felt the flush of glory when our news staff won a Pulitzer the following year. I could hardly believe I was on such a crack news team.

I'd think about Ronnie occasionally, but events would wash him out of my mind. I'd been assigned the job of investigating

Philadelphia's distressed public schools, and I spent more than a year analyzing a system of 273 schools, 224,000 students, and 26,000 employees. One of the city's oldest high schools was so dilapidated, students defecated in the hallways. Teacher absenteeism was the worst in the nation. The school superintendent faked data in his doctoral dissertation. The system was rotten.

The teachers' union was furious. On strike for fifty days that fall of 1981, they booed and spat at me as I ran alongside their protest marches, notepad in hand. A mob chanted my name outside the *Inquirer*'s towering white wedding cake of a building: "Send down Mary Bishop!" I'd been standing among them all day; they needed drama for the cameras.

I needed a long break, so I took a leave of absence from the newspaper and rented a creekside cabin in rural Rockbridge County, Virginia. It was beauty at the level of Keswick's, without the pretension. I never went back to big-city journalism. Instead, I took a job running the one-woman Lexington bureau of the *Roanoke Times & World-News*, an hour from Roanoke. My job was to cover Rockbridge and two adjacent counties. What could possibly happen there? Murder, arson, rape, drug busts, political scandals, natural disasters, all kinds of social history. I never worked so hard in my life. Astonishing things happen everywhere. Daddy taught me that, but I'd forgotten.

I BEGAN TO think more deeply about Mom and Ronnie when in 1985, Sallie Johnson Wilcher, an elderly mountain woman, introduced me to one of the cruelest chapters of American history, the eugenics movement, a twentieth-century social program that filtered individuals judged to be genetically inferior out of the breeding pool.

Beginning in the 1920s, doctors, sheriffs, and social workers in Rockbridge County and elsewhere targeted individuals they decided shouldn't reproduce. They rounded up unwed mothers like Sallie, as well as orphans, alcoholics, juvenile delinquents, and people with epilepsy, mental retardation, deformities, mental illness, and even contagious diseases such as syphilis. Authorities committed them to state hospitals, where many were sterilized and used as forced labor, sometimes for the rest of their lives.

Nazi Germany considered Virginia's eugenics law so efficient that it borrowed the law's wording to set up a system that neutered thousands before the Holocaust. My high school and college classes never mentioned this cozy relationship between Virginia and the Third Reich.

In 1929, when Sallie was nineteen and the mother of an illegitimate toddler, doctors declared her "feebleminded," a catchall label applied to a wide assortment of social undesirables. Sallie's older brother-in-law had lured her to a barn and gotten her pregnant, just like what happened to Mom. Two years later, at the instigation of Sallie's grandmother, who thought her wildness needed reining in, a welfare worker whisked away Sallie and her two-year-old son, Billy. Sallie was sterilized and put to work in the laundry of a large state mental hospital. She never saw Billy again.

Her son had died years before I met Sallie, but shortly before her death, in 1987, I learned she had three grandsons in a distant city. Billy's widow sent her the boys' pictures, along with snapshots of Billy at different ages. "Looks like his daddy," Sallie said with a wink. She nearly wore out the photos, she squinted into their faces so often.

My Sallie stories led me to other eugenics survivors. I spent

years writing about them. It could have been my mama who got locked up. She fit the formula: poor, unmarried country girl with an illegitimate baby. If she'd been targeted, I wouldn't be writing this.

WHILE IN LEXINGTON, I had a feeling Ronnie was reading my work. Occasionally I'd win an award and my picture would be in the paper. He knew I was around—I was sure of it—but he never contacted me.

As the favored child, the onus was on me to reach out to him. He must have seen that I was writing about people and events an hour or more away from him. Maybe he forgave my not coming to find him. Maybe he saw I was busy elsewhere. Then again, maybe he didn't want to see me. He might turn me away.

HE'D REAPPEARED BRIEFLY in my teens, flying up the dusty farm road in a big old car one Sunday afternoon. Ronnie was six foot four, well dressed in a shirt and tie, not bad looking in his midtwenties. His girlfriend, a six-foot-tall telephone operator, rode along. There was something of the greaser bad boy about Ronnie. His limbs sprawled casually across our couch, his long leg bones stacked against each other like firewood, he drawled with a sleazy nonchalance about cars and hunting and rambling alone through the woods. He laughed nervously. I felt a curious tension in the room. I wouldn't see Ronnie again for almost three decades.

AFTER YEARS ALONE in the Lexington bureau, I wanted company. In 1987, when I moved to the main newsroom in Roanoke, I began to think more about Ronnie. I knew he would notice from my stories that I was in town. It was time for me to find him.

Mom said his barbershop was in Vinton, a little town on Roanoke's eastern flank. I called a barber in the Yellow Pages, but he didn't know Ronnie. Another sort of recognized his name. "Ronnie Overstreet? Oh, you're talking about Slim. Yeah, he's right there on Pollard Street in Vinton. Easy to find. It's the Sportsman Barber Shop." Ronnie's place was across from the bank and the post office on Vinton's main drag.

I drove there on a September afternoon. Outside the shop door, I peered through its plate glass window. Counters of the high-ceilinged shop were piled with magazines, books, and newspapers. One person was inside—a tall man, slumped, maybe asleep, in one of two barber chairs. He didn't look familiar.

"Ronnie?" I walked tentatively through the door. He sat up, and when I saw his face, I knew it was Ronnie. He had changed, but I had trouble figuring out exactly how. He just looked odd and homely. He was staring at me, startled. I finally said, "It's Mary Carter."

"Goddamn," he said, scrambling to stand and look me over. A small smile gradually appeared around his eyes and moved to his cheeks and mouth. "Pie, what're you doing over this way?" Touchingly, affectionately, he used my childhood nickname. Judging from all the old copies of my newspaper scattered around, I knew for sure he'd been reading my stories all these years. Why had I waited so long?

In a minute, a customer slipped through the door. I settled into the line of black vinyl chairs where men waited their

turns. Ronnie's hands were masterful and quick. He could do a haircut in five minutes. In between, we got acquainted. I needed him to know how long I'd been in the dark.

"I didn't know 'til a few years ago you were my brother. I found out by accident. They said you were my cousin."

"Yeah, that's the way it was," he said, smiling awkwardly at the floor.

"I didn't find out 'til I got my birth certificate, and it said she had another kid. I should have figured it out." My voice and face dripped with apology. We fell quiet for a minute.

A state trooper rushed in for a close trim. The two talked for a half hour. I was about to burst. But Ronnie let him drone on and on about some backwoods criminals. "Those mountain people don't know any better," Ronnie told him with a knowing snicker.

After the trooper, we talked for two hours. The facts of his life began to drop into place. We didn't ask many questions of each other. We just said whatever came to mind, with him doing most of the talking. He mentioned foster parents and an orphanage.

"You had it all, kid, and I was cast off," he said, throwing his giant right hand up like he was tossing something away. He threw me a fierce look. I knew he was right, and I felt exposed. I left my raincoat on the whole time I was in the barbershop that day.

But at the same time, I could tell that Ronnie had long wished to talk with me, just as I had him. I was the one person in the world who knew all the principal players in his story.

At first, as he told me what books he read or where he went turkey hunting, he tucked his head, chin to chest, rolled his eyes way back in his head, and peered at me in the narrow

space between his glasses and his bulging brow. His eyes looked tiny behind thick black glasses much too small for his face. He looked frightening. The longer we talked, the more he lifted his head and looked me straight in the eye.

Oddly, because I could see he was a good barber, his own haircut was of the old mixing-bowl variety—straight, parted on the side, salt-and-pepper, and sticking out in sheets around his head. He obviously cut his own hair.

His voice veered from furious to tender. Trying to build some commonality, I criticized Mom's treatment of him, but he called me on it. "She had it hard, Pie." She was chased from home; she was forced to give birth among strangers in an unknown town. Our strict Methodist granddaddy did the best he could but was blinded by religion. The old man was humiliated by the sin inherent in Ronnie's birth.

Long ago, Ronnie claimed, he resigned himself to Mom's rejection. "She can't handle" was his shorthand for her shame in his birth, a sentence even he couldn't bear to complete, the unspoken "me" always hanging in the air.

Then, in a reverent tone, he posed this question: "You ever watch your mother write a letter?" Well, of course I had. Ronnie praised her "perfect" handwriting. She looked up spellings if she wasn't sure. I didn't mention how she, who dropped out of high school before becoming pregnant with him, routinely wrote "mabe" for "maybe" and "ect." instead of "etc." He took comfort in her talents and in mine and thought they were inherited.

I was always a careful speaker, taught never to cuss. I spoke like a good girl. But Ronnie inserted "damn" in nearly every sentence. A tough-guy habit, I speculated as I sat there listening. He said "nigger" a lot, hard to hear even if he was expressing

solidarity with black people as his fellow underdogs. "Just me and the niggers," he said of his callous treatment by Keswick people and those in authority elsewhere. Maybe Ronnie was why my folks freaked out so dramatically when in first grade I asked them what a "nigger" was. If Mom carried within her some evil seed, maybe it was popping up in me too.

To Ronnie, all female librarians, teachers—really, all grown women—were Old Lady So-and-So. Mom cautioned me as a child never to refer to women that way, or to men as Old Man So-and-So. Again, it must have been because Ronnie did.

He seemed to have read all my stories in the Roanoke paper. He proved it by remembering Sallie Wilcher's sterilization and the seizure of her little boy. He remembered the young punks who strangled a Roanoke hooker, lashed her nude body to the hood of their car like a deer, and drove her miles in the middle of the night before dumping her in a country stream. He'd kept up with my work, so why hadn't he called the newspaper and asked for me? "I'm your bastard brother, Pie. I didn't want to drag you down." Every advantage I'd ever had instantly felt like a minus in his column.

AS HIS TRIMMER buzzed away on a guy's crew cut, I stood up slowly and mentally compared us in the horizontal mirror that covered the wall behind the barber chairs. I was forty-two; he was fifty-two. I couldn't help but wonder if as I aged I might develop features like his. There were definite similarities—the straight hair, still some honey blond like mine in his gray; the deep-set eyes; the long, thin limbs; our family's height. But something had transformed him since his visit to the farm all those years ago.

His voice was an octave lower, raspy, with crackling mucus. His face was overgrown with flesh and bone. His fingers were strangely long and his middle fingers ended in bulbs at the tips, like spring onions. Could a car wreck have messed him up? It looked more internal, more medical. I didn't have the heart, or the nerve, to ask.

"Mary COD-ah, Mary COD-ah," he kept singsonging to himself as we talked. He said my name just the way our mother did. He was savoring the fact that I'd come.

Before I left, I handed him a business card so he'd have my phone number. He placed it delicately in front of his 1930s cash register and smiled at it. *My sister is a reporter at the biggest paper around.*

I patted him on the back. He did not respond. Hugging him seemed out of line. The stiffness of his back told me this was a man who hadn't been hugged much.

As I left, he called out, "If you need anything, you know where you can find me."

I walked to my car, out of sight, and I wept.

Later on, I called Mom to let her know I'd gone to see him. I didn't tell her much of what he said. She warned me to go slow. "Be careful. He might be putting on a good front."

THE YEAR BEFORE, she and Daddy had gone to a reunion of her Moneta School classmates. Her thick silver-blue hair set in high waves, she'd worn her most upright, upscale outfit, a pink linen suit with a silky off-white blouse and pearls. She was nervous; friends would be there, but also people she hadn't seen in fifty years. She sat primly on a folding chair, her stockinged knees squeezed tight together. Old friends came

by and hugged her, and she thought for a while that it was a good thing she'd come. But on reading her name tag, one of the other women had walked wordlessly away, and another regarded her with a frosty eye and had little to say. "They turned up their nose at me," Mom confessed to me later, her jaw twitching in a fight against tears. Maybe all of them were awkward. Maybe she imagined the contempt for which she was primed. But it didn't matter. My perfect-posture, courageous, seventy-year-old mama went there in hopes of packing away her disgrace, only to have it refreshed. She was still that frightened, humiliated, pregnant girl, Adria Overstreet.

[13]

We Get Acquainted

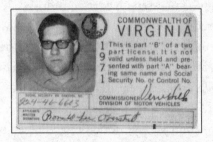

Ronnie turned thirty-six in 1971.

That year, I wrote "See Ronnie" in my datebook more than sixteen times. But I didn't go. On my 1988 calendar, I wrote his name in capital letters, with stars. I still didn't go.

I was busy, and it was hard to hear about my tenderhearted mother being so cruel to him.

My guilt mounted, and finally I started seeing him again. I went to the barbershop four more times over the next year or so. As soon as I came through the door, he'd launch into a rambling gush of story fragments and observations. He jumped from subject to subject—local pizza joints to British royalty, Vinton politics to camera lenses. He lectured me. He'd saved up insights to share with me. He was desperate to talk.

He threw college-boy words at me—"elitist," "fatalist," "utopia"—and urged me to study fifteenth-century English history as he had. Only then could I fully comprehend Virginia's pompous past. Yet his knowledge about all that seemed spotty, like a quilt missing squares. Not surprising for an eighth-grade dropout whose early schooling kept being interrupted. Still, he possessed an eager mind.

He'd visited the graves of our grandparents in country cemeteries. He'd researched the blue-blooded owners of Keswick's oldest farms. Studying the backgrounds of people from his past helped him figure out where he fit in. "That's how I found myself," he said with pride, to underscore that he had put himself in context, and nobody had helped him.

He didn't come right out and say it, but I could tell he was proud of me. He'd been following my newspaper stories. I'd won national awards and was a Pulitzer finalist for a series about how exterminators were poisoning and defrauding people. "You're the only one of us who's amounted to anything," he told me between haircuts. Sad as that statement was, at least he considered himself to be in the family "us." Every time I saw him, I wanted to cry, but not in front of him. To do that would make me more a part of his life than I was comfortable with, at least not yet.

I did what I'd learned to do as a journalist: I listened. By then, I'd been a reporter more than twenty years. I'd written about colorful strangers of all sorts in several states and cities. Ronnie was the greatest enigma of them all.

He'd lived in Virginia all his life, yet he didn't sound all that Southern. He boomed on and on in a cynical *Godfather* patois. Everything was a caper. Everybody was on the make. Men were jokers, cats, and bozos. Women were sirens if they

were good-looking, squaws if they weren't. Ronnie didn't drive his car. He wheeled his unit.

Then one day he told me that in his first barbering job, the immigrant businessmen nearby mentored him. They were from Northern cities. They became the fathers he needed; they left their imprint on him, I could hear it.

"I think the Democrats are going to nominate Jesse Jackson," I announced to him cheerfully one day in 1988. Jackson was patching together a coalition of blacks, whites, poor, rich, Northerners, Southerners, gays. I believed he could be elected. Ronnie hooted. "You kidding me? That's Mickey Mouse eating blackberries." That was my favorite comeback of his to anything he thought idealistic mush. It meant, "You're dwelling in Cartoonland, kid. The world ain't all that good."

He embraced cynicism and irreverence instead, and whenever I'd say something that rang that chime—like what a lousy job the media were doing covering the campaign—he'd snicker with glee and slowly nod his head.

IN THE YEARS when I was reconnecting with Ronnie, I ran a gantlet between him and Mom—fact-checking with her what he'd tell me and running back to him to learn more. As a sister and a daughter, I was careful—those two were wary of each other; their memories tapped a soul-close vein. Deep down, however, I remained a nosy reporter. I wanted to know every crumb of their story.

Each time I was with Ronnie, I felt worse for him and more confused about our mother. For the most part, she corroborated his accounts of events they'd shared. Each inquiry, though, seemed to ping against the lead wall she'd erected in

her mind to keep from thinking about him. Each inquiry was a small shaming by her chosen child.

But what was I going to do? Once I got to know Ronnie, I couldn't turn away. I had a right to know what had happened to my brother.

ON THANKSGIVING DAY 1988 at my folks' house in Charlottesville, Mom surprised me by phoning Ronnie out of the blue to invite him to lunch. It was late in the morning. The turkey was roasting in the oven; the potatoes were boiling in the saucepan. Ronnie lived two hours away. This was not a sincere invitation.

The young niece of Ronnie's landlady answered the phone in Vinton. She hollered up the stairs to Ronnie that a woman named Adria—Mom spelled it out—was inviting him to lunch. He shouted back that he was going hunting—probably not a sincere reply either. Ronnie's hunting expeditions started way before dawn. Mom hung up the phone, grumbling in the clumsy anger of the guilt-ridden.

At Christmas that year, Ronnie reported that she'd been writing to him. Around then, Virginia lawmakers, propelled by my reporting, were preparing massive reform to regulate pesticides. Still, her focus on me chafed Ronnie. "It's 'Mary Carter this' and 'Mary Carter that.' She don't give a damn about me."

His feelings about her were tangled and mercurial. I couldn't predict his attitude on any given day. He admired her, yet he blamed her for everything wrong in his life, and I was beginning to agree with him there. I didn't talk much about her to him. My relationship with her was so drastically different. No need to rub his nose in it.

He was unwavering, however, in his contempt for Daddy. I'd heard his recollections of Daddy not treating him right. And yet Daddy had defended Ronnie to that social worker at Western State. But Ronnie didn't know that, and I didn't either at that point. It didn't matter. I knew it was easier for Ronnie to heap blame on Daddy than to spew all his hatred at his own mother.

Somewhere under Ronnie's protective bramble of furious language, I thought I detected a kind heart. I wondered if I could fight my way through his armor and get to know that side of him. With each visit, I was beginning to put the people, places, and events of his life in chronological order.

IN AUGUST 1953, he'd stepped off a bus onto the hustle-bustle streets of downtown Roanoke. The state institutions that held him for ten months had turned him loose. They lined up a job for him. No more shock treatments. No more heavy metal doors clanging behind him. His asthma disappeared once he got away from Mom, and now the world lay before him. He had a comb in his pocket and a trade certified right there on his barber school diploma.

He'd graduated from the thousand-hour, six-month-long barbering course just down the road from Western State at the state-run Woodrow Wilson Rehabilitation Center in Fishersville, Virginia. It certified him in haircutting, shaving, shampooing, scalp treatments, massaging, barbering science, barbering ethics, and barbershop management. The day after graduation, he turned eighteen. I don't know if my folks went to the ceremony, if there even was one, or if Ronnie came home that weekend. I'd just turned eight, and I

don't remember. But days after his birthday, the state put him on that bus for Roanoke.

"I thought I'd hit the jackpot when I stepped out there on Jefferson Street and saw all those buses and trains, and all those fancy-dressed people." He'd landed a job at the epicenter of little Roanoke.

With a population of ninety-two thousand and at its all-time industrial peak, Roanoke was a three-ring circus to a restless young man. It put on a giant fair his first week there. Roanoke had seven movie theaters and more drive-ins than that. It had eateries crammed into every corner, a good public library, record stores, cute secretaries streaming by at lunchtime—Ronnie was in the catbird seat.

Europeans first called the place Big Lick for the salt marshes that conveniently drew game for them to shoot. Sodium, iron, calcium, and other nutrients in those natural "licks" strengthened animals' bones and muscles. Roanoke eventually became a manufacturing hub when railroads developed the very same trails blazed to the salty waters first by mastodons, then bison, then native people, then white settlers.

Roanoke, though a small city, was an urban oasis in the vast rural swath that is the western half of Virginia. Heading east to west across the state in the 1950s, after the capital of Richmond, you had to drive hundreds of miles to Louisville, Kentucky, to find a city bigger and livelier than Roanoke.

RONNIE'S BARBERING TEACHERS had shipped him off to work at the long-standing four-seat American Barber Shop at the corner of Jefferson Street and Campbell Avenue, Roanoke's busiest intersection. Western State didn't officially

discharge Ronnie from the hospital until March 1954 when it declared him "improved." The Roanoke job must have been granted on only a trial basis, but Ronnie stuck. He was at the American more than three years.

Though he was draft bait, he never served in the military. In October 1953, weeks after he turned eighteen and clenched that first job, the Selective Service System sent a postcard to Ronnie's rented room. The card provided him with a ten-digit identification number for the draft and directed him to notify the local draft board whenever he moved, which was often. The United States had signed an armistice that ended the Korean War slightly more than two months earlier, in late July. Either Ronnie slipped by—too young for Korea, too old for Vietnam—or his stay in a mental hospital and his electroshock there rendered him ineligible.

Fatherless Ronnie suddenly was surrounded by men of several ethnicities eager to advise the scrawny teenager on clothes, cars, money, and women. Jewish pawnbrokers, Lebanese sandwich makers, Greek hot dog vendors, Scots-Irish pool hustlers with their custom-made cue sticks—they all reached out to the solitary boy. A blend of their New York accents mixed with some Southernness—I heard it in Ronnie's voice when I finally got to know him.

A Jewish clothier with a store near the barbershop snappily outfitted Ronnie in corduroy sport coats and sharply creased gabardine slacks. Ronnie dated the daughters of downtown merchants and bragged to me that he was invited "to all the best dances."

Police took advantage of greenhorn Ronnie. "One cop liked his little nip, so I went to the liquor store for him. . . . They all got their haircuts free, and you had to buy their tickets to the

Policemen's Ball." Some leaned on him to be a snitch. "I didn't care too much for that."

He still called himself Slim, a nickname coined by the boys back at Miller School. Ronnie Overstreet was that poor bastard kid. Slim Overstreet, now, he was a man about town.

Without a car at first, he rented a room a ten-minute walk from the barbershop. The widow of a railroad machinist charged him five dollars a month for a spare room in her house. Ronnie could sit up in bed and look out across a park to the grand Tudor-style Hotel Roanoke a half mile away on the other side of the railroad tracks.

Downtown Roanoke teemed with thousands of male heads crying for regular trims. Offices in every direction from Ronnie's shop held insurance men, lawyers, railway clerks, coal dealers, telegraph operators, stockbrokers, accountants, tailors, tobacconists, real estate brokers, watch repairmen, doctors, dentists, jewelers, bankers, elevator repairmen, and shoe salesmen.

His first weekly paycheck was $35.60. After he paid for his room and for food, he had plenty of money left. "Went in the sock"—his savings. A grilled ham and cheese was $1.05 at People's Drug. He'd wolf down two. He spread his meals around town, strategically making new friends and customers. In turn, the short-order cooks, spying his thin frame, ladled on extra gravy.

In the spring of 1954, the barbershop's shoeshine guy tipped Ronnie off to a three-year-old colt running in the Belmont Stakes. The odds were fourteen to one. Ronnie went to the bookie upstairs in the pool hall and placed a week's wages on High Gun. The horse won. Thirty years later, Ronnie still was savoring the memory of his good fortune. "I left out of the pool hall that day with a grocery sack *full* of money."

He went car shopping. The first used-car dealer called him a hayseed, so Ronnie moved on. At the next place, he discovered a '49 Buick, a preacher's car, jet-black, spotless. He paid $1,300 for it, most of his winnings. "A cigarette had never been smoked in it, and along comes Slim." Now, not only could Ronnie peer out his bedroom window and admire Roanoke's finest hotel, he could look down on the street and see his very own car. He washed it weekly and faithfully changed its oil.

As he stood on the corner outside the barbershop during a break one day, old tycoon J.J. McIntyre cruised by. Ronnie's boyhood pal Buddy McIntyre, a teenager by then, couldn't get his granddad to stop. For years after, Ronnie relished the memory of Buddy, ecstatic to see his old friend, waving like mad and leaning halfway out the window of "that goddamned Mercury." Ronnie's new roots in Roanoke were not only fattening him up and making him smile but also healing old wounds.

THE BARBERSHOP WAS the scene of one of the most dramatic events in Ronnie's life. I heard two versions.

As Ronnie recalled, it was around lunchtime when a thin brown-haired man slipped into his chair for a cut. Within seconds, Ronnie realized he was intimately familiar with that head. He glanced in the mirror and saw the long face of his foster father, Roy Hall. Ronnie hadn't seen Polly and Roy for more than ten years, not since he left Boys' Home.

In an undated letter I found in Ronnie's file at the orphanage, Polly wrote, "My dear little boy, guess you think I am not going to ever answer your sweet letter but it has been so hot and everything that I just haven't felt like writing. I surely

hope you are being extra nice so you can come over next week for your vacation. Please try to be good and not get any bars," which were Boys' Home's version of demerits. She signed off, "Love always, Mother."

Ronnie often left Boys' Home to spend holidays back in Blacksburg with Polly and Roy. But once he checked out of the orphanage at age eight and joined Mom at Bridlespur, Polly and Roy decided to butt out and to let Ronnie settle in with her. Little did they know how badly that was going.

Ronnie thought for years about reconnecting with Polly and Roy. But he was afraid. He never understood why he had to leave them in the first place. Had he done something wrong? Had they stopped loving him? He had no idea that they'd begged Mom for years to let them adopt him.

As Ronnie scissored Roy's hair, Roy began to chat about this and that. Ronnie, so tall now that Roy didn't recognize him, was about to pop with excitement. Finally, Ronnie casually remarked, "Didn't you have a little blond-headed boy years ago?" Roy blanched and asked, "Hey, yeah. How'd you know that?" To which Ronnie replied, "Because you're talking to him."

Roy leapt up and wrapped Ronnie in his arms. After a minute, Roy wagged his finger at Ronnie, just like he was his little boy all over again. *Now, you wait right here, okay? I'm going to go get Polly. Don't you go anywhere!* Roy sped the fifty miles home and was back with Polly by two o'clock. There was so much hugging and kissing that the whole barbershop was celebrating with them. So, as Ronnie recalled fondly, "There was nothing to do but take the rest of the day off."

Polly's memory was that Ronnie had cut the hair of a friend of Roy's who told Roy about this young Roanoke

barber named Ronnie who knew all about Roy. "Roy came home. He was all upset. He told me, 'We're going to Roanoke tomorrow.'" She rode along and they were all reunited at the barbershop.

Regardless of how exactly it happened, that day reassured Ronnie of Polly and Roy's affections, and if he had any lingering doubts, they were dispatched the following Sunday, when Polly's whole family welcomed him back into their fold. The clan put on a feast and mounted a banner out front: "Welcome home, Ronnie." He found old pictures of himself in every room of Polly and Roy's house, and a fat album of his childhood photos set out on a table. It was one of the happiest days of his life.

For the next five years, Ronnie drove his Buick to Blacksburg most weekends. He wasn't much of a churchgoing fellow, but for Polly and Roy's sake he tagged along with them to services. Ronnie's father figures back in Roanoke had advised him to find his girlfriends in church, not bars. "Church," they'd counseled him, "is where you'll find the clean girls."

Polly became his mother all over again. He complained to her about how my folks spoiled me and neglected him. "We shamed him about being jealous of you," she told me. "We told him, well, that you were his mother's only girl and he was her boy that had been away from her so much and had taken other people into his life. That was all right; she still loved him too."

About 1957, Ronnie left Roanoke. The American Barber Shop, in business downtown since the twenties, disappeared from city directories. So did the building it inhabited. Ronnie moved a couple of counties away to Buck's Barber Shop on Main Street in Lexington, Virginia. With two nearby colleges

associated with Confederate generals, Robert E. Lee's Washington and Lee and Thomas J. "Stonewall" Jackson's Virginia Military Institute, Ronnie could snip hair all day and absorb history from Lexington's patriarchal old guard. He rented a room above Main Street.

As in Roanoke, mentors popped up, prime among them the late Leon C. Johenning, a nationally known turkey-hunting writer and producer of handmade wood-and-metal turkey calls, tiny boxes that in the hands of a deft user could cluck, purr, and cackle just like a hen to draw a big, prize tom. From him, Ronnie learned about turkey hunting.

Ronnie began buying guns and renting hunting lodges with other men to hunt turkeys and other wildlife on the weekends. Leon eventually shot more turkey pictures than actual birds. Under his tutelage, Ronnie bought a camera and became a nature lover like Leon, exploring the mountains of Virginia and West Virginia, often alone, on his days off.

He was most intrigued by the oldest forests, where sycamores once measured forty-five feet around and where the wood from just one of those mammoths might fill an entire log train. Ronnie hiked alone into a national forest and waded across a river to an abandoned lumber camp and emerged with a prize—one of the numbered metal discs immigrant lumberjacks pinned to their clothes or wore on leather thongs around their necks as identification. At back-roads shops along his drives, Ronnie snapped up McGuffey Readers and other old books and antiques for a song and sold them at a profit to collectors.

In 1958, Ronnie pocketed a handsome raise when he moved to George's Barbershop in Buena Vista, a small industrial town set against the Blue Ridge Mountains a few miles from

Lexington. He began campaigning for Polly and Roy to let him return home. Neither were feeling well, and one visit became particularly strained. "He begged the whole weekend to come back, and we told him, well, he could always come whenever he wanted to [but] that he was a grown man now and could take care of himself . . . But just to give up his job and come, I said, 'Don't do that.'" Polly was caring for her mother, who was blind, and babysitting a niece. She had all she could handle.

Back in Blacksburg in March 1959, Roy Hall dropped dead in his garage. Ronnie went to his funeral, and there, among the friends and neighbors who came by the Halls' bungalow after the service, Ronnie met his first serious girlfriend, a seventeen-year-old high school senior Polly and Roy knew through their church. Ronnie was twenty-three. He would date the girl for more than a year, but he lost touch with Polly. He felt her Christianity was turning too strident.

He'd heard that an old barber in Vinton was looking for a second-chair man at Phillips Barber Shop. Vinton was an easygoing little town of eight thousand hitched to Roanoke's eastern hip. It was a working person's quiet Mayberry, with a textile mill and lots of guys in need of conservative haircuts. The shop, in the heart of town, had a classy feel, with lots of light and ten-foot ceilings in patterned plaster. Ronnie earned his highest wages yet and rented a room nearby, where he'd serve his girlfriend lunch and fizzy nonalcoholic drinks.

Old Man Phillips, as Ronnie called Hubert Phillips behind his back, disciplined Ronnie professionally and otherwise. He pushed Ronnie to attend his Methodist church for Sunday school and worship. Ronnie and his girlfriend sat in the front row at eleven o'clock services. Soon, though, Ronnie and the

girl split up, a hurt that remained lodged in Ronnie's heart for the rest of his life.

Early in the 1960s, he rented a bedroom and adjoining kitchenette on Vinton's hilltop Halliahurst Avenue. It was where the higher-ups lived, except that in Vinton, with few truly rich people, the higher-ups were bookkeepers, salesmen, an accountant, a teacher, a cafeteria manager, and a welder. For Ronnie, it was the Vinton equivalent of moving into the big house.

A widow named Maggie Booth rented two of her thirteen rooms to Ronnie. With her children gone, she treated him like a son and a helpmate. He did chores and feasted on Maggie's home-butchered chickens and pigs, her homemade butter and biscuits, and apple butter and cherry jam made from her orchard. Maggie died, and all of a sudden, Ronnie was sharing the house with one of Maggie's daughters-in-law, Maxine, a short, vivacious weaver at the textile mill.

I'll never know the full nature of Ronnie's relationship with Maxine, but Ronnie adored her. He called her Max—or Keys, she had so many of them. Sixteen years Ronnie's senior, Maxine was like a generous big sister. She made banana splits for them. She caught the breeze with him on the front porch summer evenings and watched *The Love Boat* and *The Dukes of Hazzard* with him winter nights. He mowed her grass, changed her oil, and made her feel secure. If he wanted to draw closer, he was reluctant. He could risk losing his cozy home if things went sour, and being a pessimist, he figured they would. He'd better play it safe.

Instead, he dated Annie, that tall telephone operator he'd brought to the farm that one time I'd seen him when I was a teenager. She had a son from an early marriage, and Ronnie

mentally compared his childhood with that of Annie's little boy. The child had all the attention, toys, and food Ronnie never got from Mom, yet the kid wasn't satisfied and, when grown, rolled in and out of prison for thefts and other crimes.

Annie, jealous of Maxine, pressed Ronnie for a commitment. "She wanted *more*." He'd spend a day and most of a night with Annie, then go home to Maxine's. Annie wanted to marry him. He briefly moved out of Maxine's and in with Annie, but he wasn't able to give himself fully to her. He felt more comfortable keeping one foot out the door in case somebody was about to boot him. He moved back in with Maxine, and Annie married another man.

On a solitary hike one weekend, Ronnie ran across a hermit living high in the mountains of Botetourt County, near Roanoke. Long before his choices became socially acceptable, even hip, Will Sloan lived off the grid, ate native plants to cure his ills, feasted on wild game, and grew his black hair and beard halfway down his chest.

Privacy-prizing Will nearly shot Ronnie's head off the first time Ronnie stumbled onto his log house on Garden Mountain, a rocky three-thousand-foot summit slithering with rattlesnakes. Thereafter, when Ronnie was coming up, he'd mail a postcard in advance. Will earned a living digging up the fleshy roots of ginseng, a reputed aphrodisiac popular around the world. His outdoor easy chair was a fat log into which he'd chiseled a depression for his butt. He attached wooden arms to his mountain throne and sat there entertaining Ronnie with stories about how to domesticate a bear cub and how to tenderize the meat of the uncooperative ones. Will was wise, hilarious, tough, and thoroughly independent, just like Ronnie dreamed of being.

In 1967, Ronnie's boss retired at sixty-five. For $647, Ronnie acquired the business, a revolving barber pole, barber chairs, an adding machine, a gas stove, a water heater, mirrors, lights, a snow shovel, and an awning over the door. He renamed the rented place the Sportsman Barber Shop.

Ronnie possessed serious spending money now. He squired girlfriends around a rustic nineteenth-century lake resort atop a peak near Blacksburg. He'd learned his way around the place through his friendship with the stable man, who gleaned a case of beer from Ronnie on every visit.

Down in Vinton, the town's male muckety-mucks—lawyers, bankers, state legislators—all streamed into the Sportsman, along with highway pavers and garbage haulers. It was one of the few places in town where a guy could find the *Wall Street Journal*. One of Ronnie's all-time favorite "heads," as he called his customers, was Homer Hopper, an up-by-his-bootstraps executive who traveled the world setting up textile mills. Every Christmas for years, Ronnie had dinner with Homer and his wife, Bertha, who made sure there was a jar of homemade jelly or a little something under the tree for him.

The Hoppers' son, Al, became one of the few close friends Ronnie ever had. Ronnie was at his best with Al and got to rattle around like a big dog, something like the powerful Keswick pooh-bahs he'd once envied. Ronnie and Al bought tickets to golf tournaments at the Homestead and Greenbrier resorts in the Appalachian Mountains, where prosperous people had been gathering for two centuries and where the two guys joked their way into the VIP lounges, replete with cigars, shrimp cocktails, and rich women.

Eventually, Al moved away, first to Houston, then to Richmond, and founded a small chain selling architectural and en-

gineering supplies. Two or three times, Ronnie visited Al and his wife at their home in an affluent Richmond suburb. At the end of the day, Ronnie would sleep in his car in the Hoppers' driveway rather than use their nicely appointed guest room. "I couldn't get him to come in the house and go to bed," Al recalled. "He didn't want to impose on anybody." Sadder yet, Ronnie probably didn't feel worthy of the guest room, even at his best friend's house.

RONNIE EMBARKED ON a self-improvement course. With the help of librarians and his better-educated customers, he devised a history curriculum for himself. He trudged around cemeteries in Bedford County to the graves of his Overstreet and McLain ancestors. He read thick histories of Bedford County, Mom's home, and the counties all around. Through history books, he came to understand the haughty attitudes of Virginia's first English-born lords and ladies and the servility of the indentured Irish, Scottish, and English immigrants who were his forebears.

Many of Ronnie's readings dripped with white supremacy, and yet he also sought out Black Power writers of the sixties and seventies. He read Eldridge Cleaver, H. Rap Brown, and Malcolm X. He connected with what they said about how at the root of racial bigotry was a social class struggle that had ensnared poor people of all races since the beginning of this country. Powerful white men had always ruled with an unflinching fist. Ronnie had seen that for himself in Keswick.

He preferred reading about the little guys—the ingenious slaves, hillbillies, American Indians, and frontiersmen who knew this country best and whose knowledge of its natural

systems was overpowered by industrial greed. Ronnie considered himself one of those clever survivors. Louis L'Amour's frontier sagas traced Ronnie's favorite fictional family, the Sacketts, as they hunted for treasure, mined for gold, fought mountain lions, and dug ginseng, just as Will Sloan still did.

EACH DAY AT the barbershop, Ronnie absorbed his customers' stories and those they recalled from their great-grandpas. Even though his heads enriched his knowledge, Ronnie liked to rag on the monotony of how he made his living. "Cuttin' heads, cuttin' heads," was his lament. "I am an ear," he'd wearily tell his friends, complaining about the more boring stuff he was forced to listen to. But he fell into a slump each time illness or injury barred him from his hair-snipping station at the Sportsman.

Back in the fifties, during his final months at Western State, when administrators were trying to figure out what to do with Ronnie, his therapist told him about the different kinds of state training available to him. Ronnie could have become a welder. He could have been a watch repairman. He chose barbering.

The other trades would have been solitary, but in Ronnie's otherwise lonely life, barbering fed him a regular, predictable intimacy that was tactile and friendly yet not so intrusive as to be threatening. Except for his customers' occasional thank-you handshakes or slaps on the back, Ronnie did all the touching, on his terms, dozens of times a day.

By the time Ronnie and I got reacquainted, he'd been barbering more than thirty years. The instant a man or boy plopped down in his chair, Ronnie launched movements that composed a rhythmic song. He'd open his big right hand and,

palm-down, whack a vertical hydraulic pump to adjust the chair's height and lock it into position. *Thud-click-bump*, Ronnie's motions sent the man sharply to the left and back in two seconds and said without his speaking, *Hey, bub, hold on for the ride. Stay still and don't mess with Slim Overstreet.* He'd swish the brown plastic drape up into the air, toreador-style, so that it fluttered down perfectly over the man's lap and shoulders. Next, he snapped open a white paper collar and deftly placed it around the guy's neck so trimmings wouldn't sift under his shirt. Then came the comb, the scissors, and the chatter. Ronnie was so big, his voice so deep, some men looked a little intimidated.

Ronnie's prices were on his secret sliding scale, zero bucks to five depending on what you could afford and how much he liked you, and he was attentive to all his heads. He'd cultivated them from the time their mamas brought them in as toddlers. When a boy was getting his first cut, Ronnie softened the trauma by letting him reach into big jars of coins to buy candy and ice cream down the street. The nerviest kids reached into his cash register and grabbed greenbacks. Ronnie always let it go. He figured it was a long-term investment. Sure enough, years later a guy walked into the barbershop and plopped down a twenty-dollar bill. He'd stolen five dollars from his old barber as a kid and wanted to make it right.

Longtime heads wondered why Ronnie looked increasingly odd, but few of them said anything. By the eighties, he was reminding a few heads of the tall, big-browed manservant on the sixties sitcom *The Addams Family*. Ronnie grunted and scowled when those newer heads started calling him Lurch.

What Was Wrong

Ronnie's driver's license photos, showing the
growth of his facial features, provided unintended
documentation of his disease.

I was reading in bed when my phone rang at ten thirty on
a Tuesday night. A newspaper editorial assistant was re-
laying a telephone message from a woman looking for Ron-
nie Overstreet's sister. The caller couldn't remember my
name. All she knew was that I was a reporter. The editorial
assistant pieced it together.

It was Ronnie's landlady and good friend, Maxine Booth.
She was frantic. The Vinton First Aid Crew had just taken
Ronnie to Community Hospital of Roanoke Valley. He was
in grave condition.

I'd never met Maxine. She'd gone away for a long week-
end, and when she returned home that Monday afternoon in

April 1990, she heard labored breathing from within Ronnie's bedroom. The door was chain-locked from the inside. After much pleading by Maxine, Ronnie came to the door in his underwear, then collapsed on the floor. For almost ten hours, he refused to let her call the rescue squad. "Hell, no!" he thundered. Finally, just before she dialed the newspaper, he let them come. Maxine was exhausted, and fearful. She didn't drive at night. "You need to go to the hospital, Mary. He might not make it."

I threw on clothes and flew out the door. I'd known all along that something was wrong with Ronnie. But I kept my distance and didn't ask about his health. Before I could see him that night, doctors told me that by the time paramedics reached Ronnie, he'd passed out again. He was dehydrated from days of respiratory distress. His blood pressure was 240/140, high enough to bring on kidney failure or a stroke.

Once he came to, he told the staff he hadn't eaten for days. In the emergency room, they inserted a plastic tube in his throat to make sure he could breathe. He yanked the tube out a little while later in intensive care. Staff tied his hands and feet and reinserted the tube. In the space for family contacts on his hospital admission form, somebody typed in capital letters, "NO ONE."

By the time I got there, Ronnie was sleeping and stable, so I went home and napped for a couple of hours. Right before I got back early the next morning, doctors tried to pull the tube out to see if he could breathe without it. His throat snapped shut. Ronnie panicked. I watched terrified through the window of the door as Ronnie bucked like a horse and the team of eight—doctors, nurses, an anesthesiologist, and a surgeon—struggled to reinsert the tube. They gave him Valium,

and when he woke up banging his tied arms on the bed rails, more Valium.

As I walked down a hallway, one of the medical residents asked if I knew what was wrong with Ronnie. I said no, that we'd just gotten reacquainted after a lifetime apart. I couldn't figure out why he'd changed so much since I knew him as a child. It took only three words to solve the mystery. "He has acromegaly," the doctor said. I'd never heard the word.

Ronnie had a tiny benign tumor, little bigger than a postage stamp, on his pituitary gland. He'd had it for at least twenty years. The condition, acromegaly, had stimulated the gland to produce growth hormones that caused Ronnie's forehead, nose, mouth, hands, feet, and heart to grow. The disorder led to shrinkage of his airways. It had nearly squeezed the life out of him. Normal growth hormones in an adult measure around eight. Ronnie's were fifty in the first hospital test and, later that day, seventy-two.

Now it all made sense. After each time I'd seen Ronnie, I'd tried to explain to Mom and my friends how something was deforming him. I'd never seen anything like it.

The doctor said they could have stopped Ronnie's acromegaly years ago, before it did most of its damage to his body, but no one was there with Ronnie to wonder what was wrong. Where was I in all this? Our mother? She'd seen him in the 1970s, and wondered, too, why he looked the way he did. But we were guarded around him. We hadn't pressed the issue. Neither had Maxine.

In my first phone talks with Maxine, I zeroed in on her as my scapegoat. She sounded fake sweet. "He's like one of the family," she kept saying in her little-girl voice. "My whole family thinks the world of him." She emphasized that she

never went inside Ronnie's bedroom, just down the hall from hers. "He's a very private person." She knew he was living "clean and right," though, and that's why she welcomed him to stay on after her husband died seventeen years before.

Ronnie had told me about mowing Maxine's yard and doing chores around her house. He sounded like a new version of a tenant farmer to me, like our kin. As my mind raced for answers, I blamed Maxine for Ronnie's troubles. I imagined that she'd held him in some nagging system of peonage, a free room for his labors, and he'd never been able to set himself free. She'd kept him from getting out and making the close friends who might have urged him to get help for his condition.

Finally, with the breathing tube reinserted, nurses untied Ronnie's hands. He couldn't talk. His eyes were wild. He mouthed words I couldn't make out. Eventually, we got him a pen and paper. He wanted me to know that he had health insurance and that he had $20,000 in Southwest Virginia Savings and Loan in downtown Roanoke. He must have thought he might die there in the hospital, because he was most determined to tell me that he had life insurance too and that he had cash hidden at Maxine's house.

I was keeping Mom posted. That Wednesday, Ronnie's second day in the hospital, she and Daddy arrived at the ICU. It was their forty-eighth wedding anniversary and the first time they'd seen Ronnie in years.

I was seated in a chair by his bed when they slipped quietly through the door. Over the heaves and sighs of the machines helping him, Ronnie heard his mother's voice. Standing there in her mauve London Fog raincoat, she greeted him apprehensively, "Hi, Ronnie." His eyes shot over to her, and to Daddy, standing beside her with his arms behind his back, hanging

his head a little. I kept my eyes at the foot of the bed, at Ronnie's blood pressure readout on the portable vitals cart. It was 200/115 and climbing.

Ronnie was still smarting from the last trip he made to Mom and Daddy's at Bridlespur in 1976. Daddy had asked him then, "Ronnie, what do you want?" Ronnie thought Daddy was implying he'd come to ask for money, which Ronnie had never done and was too proud to do under any circumstances. The question infuriated and humiliated him. I don't think he confronted Early about it at the time, or ever, but Ronnie never forgot the perceived slight. I had asked my folks about that day. Both recalled Daddy asking the question. They insisted that what Daddy meant was "What do you want *out of life*?" That struck me as lame. Whatever Daddy meant, he should have known it would hurt Ronnie. The rip in Ronnie's relationship with my folks widened even more after that.

Now, in the ICU, I could feel that their presence was so stressful to Ronnie that it could kill him. My brother, who would only present himself to them in an optimal state—finest clothes, shoes shined, hair freshly cut, car waxed to high gloss, statuesque girlfriend by his side—was laid out there at his most vulnerable. He was in no condition to entertain the nemeses of his life. I had to get them out of there. I whispered that we should go. They, as well as Ronnie, were visibly relieved.

That evening, Mom and I finally met Maxine and saw where Ronnie lived. We went to the house, as the doctors had suggested, to retrieve his wallet, his identification cards, and any documentation of health insurance. Ronnie also wanted me to gather whatever cash I could find and to keep it safe for him.

I still didn't trust Maxine. Why was Ronnie so nervous

about leaving money in her house? But she actually seemed like a pleasant woman. She was short, plump, with reddish-brown hair and warm blue eyes. She unlocked Ronnie's two rooms, which she referred to as his "apartment." Clothes were piled four feet high around his bedroom. An interior doorway just past his disheveled bed led to the sort of kitchenette— refrigerator, small sink, stove—homeowners installed long ago so they could rent out a room. Ronnie had no bathroom of his own. He shared one down the hall with Maxine.

Mom, still in her raincoat, followed Maxine and me silently into Ronnie's chamber. Her mouth hanging open, her eyes rapidly blinking, she looked around at the filthy bed linens and the heaps of paper, trash, and shoes scattered around the floor. This was her child's home, a dysfunctional, dirty mess.

As Maxine looked on, I searched through a stack of down vests I'd spotted in a corner on the floor. Ronnie said he'd stashed money in a vest, but I found no money there. I grabbed the khaki pants he'd worn before the rescue squad came. Back at my house, I searched the contents of his pants pockets. I found his wallet, five driver's licenses, some small folded papers, and $5,800 in cash. Ronnie had been walking around with more money than I'd put down on my house. That was the night I found the banded stack of Mom's long-ago letters and birthday cards.

Mom and I returned to the hospital for an evening meeting with the doctors. At a desk in a room down the hall from Ronnie, I lined up in chronological order the pictures I'd just found in Ronnie's room: Ronnie at three, then at around twenty-five, then his driver's license photos throughout the seventies and eighties. Snips of hair from Ronnie's customers had wandered from his hands to his pockets and his wallet,

and now they sifted down onto the desk. In the photos, we witnessed a painful march of bone and flesh across Ronnie's face. One of the doctors quietly mumbled, awestruck, "Watch it grow."

We saw how the acromegaly gradually expanded his jawbone and lengthened his chin by inches. His forehead bulged; his lips blew up. What we couldn't see in the photos was that his teeth had separated. His hands were widening. His middle fingers bulbed out at their tips like little lightbulbs. At age fifty-four, his feet were still growing. I made a mental note of the small mountain of old shoes I'd just glimpsed in his bedroom.

A few years before the disease finally sent Ronnie to the hospital, a survey of acromegaly patients found that on average they lived with symptoms eight to ten years before they received a diagnosis. Ronnie had put up with warning signs for at least twice that long. His diagnosis came only when he nearly died.

Usually a man Ronnie's age had a wife and children to wonder why he kept outgrowing his shoes and why his facial features kept changing. Nearly everyone with the disorder seeks help and halts its progression. That's why Ronnie, with late-stage acromegaly, was so unusual. The youngest doctors standing beside Mom and me in the hospital that night had only read about acromegaly in textbooks. They'd never seen it in person, much less such an advanced case.

They explained to us that when a person develops a pituitary tumor before puberty, the legs and arms keep growing and the patient might become a giant. Ronnie may have been as tall as six foot five at one point—his height measurements vary throughout his records—but he was not a giant. He was

an Overstreet, and we tend to be tall. His tumor came along after puberty, when the long bones of his limbs had fused. Therefore, his overgrowth concentrated in the bones of his hands, feet, and face and in his organs and soft tissues.

Quickly I was absorbing the medical reasons for two of Ronnie's traits that long had baffled me—that deeper-than-ever voice and his persistent joint pain. Acromegaly reshapes the larynx, deepens the voice, and enlarges air cavities in the cranial bones, all of which gave Ronnie's voice a deep, gravelly, hollow-sounding resonance, a basso profundo that boomed as from the bottom of a well. Between customers in the barbershop, he would flex his shoulders violently—shoulders in, shoulders out, like a bird repeatedly pushing back its wings. Now I learned that painful overgrowths at the shoulders, hips, knees, and back are common with acromegaly.

MOM HAD BEEN in such a rush to leave home that day that she'd forgotten to grab her Ativan, the antianxiety drug she'd become addicted to since she was forced off Bridlespur eight years earlier. One of the doctors called in some to my pharmacy so she could sleep that night. With all this terrible news about Ronnie, she was a wreck. She stumbled around my house like a zombie, groaning as though she hurt, and then she blurted out, "Mary Carter, I told you who Ronnie was." When I was little, she'd revealed to me that he was my brother, but I was too young to understand. She never mentioned it to me again.

Mom and Daddy drove back to Charlottesville the following morning. From then on, it was just Ronnie and me, side by side in the hospital for the next thirty-seven days. In between

his medical crises, whenever the plastic tube was out of his throat and he could talk, he spat out more of his story, and I began to deal with my conflicting feelings about him. I was fascinated with Ronnie the story. But what about Ronnie the man?

I THOUGHT EVERYTHING would get better now that he'd been diagnosed. That's the way doctors were laying it out for us. That, I guess, was what they were hoping for.

On his fourth day in the hospital, after the tracheal tube came out without complications and he could talk again, I began to share with him what I was learning about his hormonal disease. Doctors had explained the basics to me, and now I was reading about it on my own at lunchtime—at the newspaper and in the library. It was believed that only forty people in a million worldwide had it.

Ronnie stared at me, expressionless, as I explained his symptoms to him and the solution the doctors were proposing.

A pituitary neurosurgeon could take most of the tumor out fairly easily, not by cutting into Ronnie's head but by threading a slender instrument through his nose or under his upper lip to reach the pituitary through the sphenoid sinus behind his nose. I told Ronnie that once the tumor was plucked, his feet and hands would stop growing. Some of the soft-tissue growth, such as that of his heart, larynx, tongue, nose, and lips, would gradually subside. He would breathe more easily; he would sleep more soundly. His protruding brow, however, and his long jaw and his big hands and feet were permanently his.

Most urgent was the need to get the tumor out and away

from his optic nerve. Doctors were warning that the tumor was already pressing on the nerve. A few more nanometers of tumor growth could snuff out the paired optic nerve to his eyes and blind him instantly. Heroic notions swirled in my brain. I was going to make up for all the neglect of his life. I was going to save him. I would compensate for my childless years and become the mother he'd never had.

Ronnie had listened patiently. Then I heard the first inklings of denial welling up in him. "Oh, I'm getting better. It's not that bad." Yes, he acknowledged, his shoe size had crept from 12 to 13 to 14, but he thought his feet were no longer growing so quickly. He was pleased about that. It wasn't easy finding shoes larger than size 14.

Ronnie's many doctors, especially the gland specialists, the endocrinologists, were in and out of his hospital room for five weeks. They studied his blood hormones; they looked at his tumor through magnetic resonance imaging, and with his permission, they photographed him. To them, Ronnie was a medical star. Ronnie would ask intelligent questions of them. He'd listen to them earnestly. Then, as soon as they were out of earshot, he'd turn a jaded face to me and laugh. "This is all a bunch of bullshit."

One day, a visiting pituitary specialist came to his room and laid out a plan. I was excited. At that time, no surgeon in Roanoke had the experience to remove the tumor. So their first idea was to send him for surgery at George Washington University Hospital in Washington, D.C.; Ronnie nodded. He seemed receptive to the idea. But as soon as the doctor left, Ronnie smart-assed to me, "Yeah, then Ethiopia, Bangkok, and Zululand."

Going to some big city for surgery struck Ronnie as a

high-flown lark. Out screeched a smart-ass voice of my own: "Slim, they're trying to help you."

"Yeah, easy for them to come up with all these cockeyed schemes. Won't be their ass going up there to be cut on."

He privately spouted a bouquet of reasons for his symptoms. He simply looked like the people of Appalachia, who seemed odd to city people but whose ugliness was common in the mountains. Or he'd explain away his condition by saying simply, "I'm a freak." One of his doctors was black. Ronnie said he identified with the man. "I know what it's like to be the only one who looks like me in a room."

Then there was Ronnie's most bizarre theory, mentioned to me more than once: Somehow all his ailments were a conspiracy to punish him for not taking sides in that fall's vote on a merger of Roanoke City with Roanoke County. Ronnie recalled a female teller at the bank across from the barbershop laughing and telling him, "Well, you won't be driving long." Ronnie interpreted her remark as some sort of threat from the Vinton establishment. This was so crazy that I had no comeback.

Nor did I have one for the most heartbreaking explanation he offered for his condition: "I just look like my old man, whoever the hell he was."

THAT AFTERNOON, I rode with him in an ambulance to an imaging center a mile away. Doctors needed to confirm that he had a pituitary tumor and to measure its proximity to other vital structures inside his head. The radio waves of magnetic resonance imaging could reveal in detail all the features inside his skull.

As the heavy door to the MRI room closed solidly behind Ronnie and the aide who would position him, the technician invited me to sit with him in the control room. Through a wide, thick window into the MRI room, I watched the aide's difficulty getting Ronnie to lie flat on the scanner bed. Ronnie yelped in pain. His mangled right hip and leg, healed crooked after a long-ago fall off a railroad trestle, made it agonizing for him to recline on a hard surface. But for images to be captured clearly, he needed to lie there and hold himself still for quite a few minutes. Once Ronnie settled down, a nurse injected him with Magnevist, or gadopentetate dimeglumine, a drug that clarifies images of abnormalities inside the cranium.

At the control panel, the technician wasn't allowed (or qualified) to tell me what the pictures were showing on the monitor, although he did point out the pituitary. In images of Ronnie's head taken straight ahead and to the side, I saw an irregularly shaped lump clinging to the tiny gland. After all these years, the tumor was only the size of a Coca-Cola cap. It measured 3 × 2.5 × 2.2 centimeters, large among acromegaly patients.

A few days later, a radiologist's report confirmed what all Ronnie's symptoms, his blood tests, and his startling appearance had already indicated: Ronnie did have acromegaly.

BACK IN HIS hospital room, Ronnie told me he thought he recognized one of the MRI guys as somebody he'd seen in Vinton. The man was yet another character in Ronnie's conspiracy theory. He seemed to think he'd been kidnapped by the rescue squad and was being held captive at the hospital. Now I was questioning Ronnie's sanity.

He bragged to me about "riding the MRI." It was hot inside that tubelike machine. It banged and clattered like a jackhammer. "I did it to satisfy a whim," he said with teasing annoyance. "*Yours.*"

He wasn't buying any of this crap about some mumbo jumbo called acro-whatever-it-was.

"You know they're just trying to help you, right?" I said.

Ever the wise guy, he replied, "Help themselves to my bank account, you mean." I was the spoiled kid who trusted people; he was the neglected kid who didn't.

Ronnie might have been paranoid, but his irreverence often made me laugh. The fervent Christians who swarmed the hospital especially got his goat. A young Baptist preacher grasping a Bible made his proselytizing round on the ward one day, asking Ronnie, "Have you surrendered to the Lord for your salvation?"

"Naw," Ronnie shot back lackadaisically. "Haven't gotten around to it."

DURING THOSE WEEKS in the hospital Ronnie told me the worst things from his childhood. That was when he told me our mother warned him at age eight, after he arrived in Keswick, never to call her Mama. That was when he told me he had electroshock therapy at Western State. Every night I went home with ever darker information about him and about my family. That I was aghast at all this surprised Ronnie. "I never thought you'd give a damn about me," he said, giving me the rare look straight in the eye.

"You know," I told him, "I owe you for all the good stuff

that's happened to me. You were her first kid. She wanted to do better the second time. I got everything you didn't."

He snorted. "You got that right."

MY OPENING UP like that unlocked his trust, as well as his mouth. Some days he talked to me for five hours straight. When the nurses bathed him or took him away for tests, I'd go to the waiting room at the end of the hall and write down everything he'd said.

AFTER RONNIE'S FIRST week in the hospital, I'd already listened to him so many hours that I was exhausted. I was home only long enough to feed my cats and sleep a little. I was overidentifying with Ronnie. I'd seen every square inch of him by then, and my feet, legs, all of me, felt like his. We shared the enlarged, arthritic Overstreet knees and the long, thin thighs of our mama and our grandpa. I felt Ronnie's brow superimposed over mine. He and I shared the same sour smell of our oily skin. Even my sebaceous glands were kin to Ronnie's.

I was determined not to abandon him in the hospital. Martyr-like, I was appropriating our mother's guilt in not caring for him. Here was a chance to use my reservoir of nurturing on my mixed-up brother.

At times while taking Ativan for his anxieties, he became docile and even lovable. He expressed sincere thanks to the nurses. "Thank you, dear," he'd say as they padded in and out. Some of them and the youngest doctors had been afraid of him earlier when he'd pounded those giant hands on the side rails.

One of his many symptoms was a thickening of skin on his heels. It was a wrestling match to get those tight rubber-bottomed hospital socks over his oversized heels. He thanked me for doing that and for bringing him little tubs of sherbet from the fridge at the nurses' station.

IT HADN'T YET been three years since I first reconnected with Ronnie, and I hadn't told him much about myself. In the hospital, I began to fill in the details. For instance, Mom had never told him why they'd left Bridlespur. I explained that Anne McIntyre Black had fired Daddy and evicted my folks from the farm.

"Mom had kind of a nervous breakdown. We couldn't get her off the couch. She'd lie there for hours and just cry. Remember what a speed demon Uncle Albert was? They took a little trip with him right around then. Mom was in the back seat and could see the speedometer. She had a panic attack in a little town. They thought she was having a heart attack and pulled over. She saw a doctor who put her on Ativan. She's tried and tried to get off it, but she's never been able to." Ronnie was hanging on my every word.

I described the day I was back home to help the folks pack up the farmhouse. Daddy and I were gathering his tools down by the dairy barn when Mrs. McIntyre (we still called her that) and her new husband drove slowly by in their station wagon. "She gave us a little wave from the passenger seat, like Queen Elizabeth parading by the peons," I told him, gesturing as she had. "I jammed my hands deep in my jeans pockets and glared at her. They drove on off."

After I'd finished, Ronnie looked me hard in the eye for

a few seconds. Then, with the most malevolent face I'd ever seen on him (and I'd seen plenty), he croaked, "Would you like to see that place *burn*?" He drew the word out so menacingly that it had flames licking off it. It took me a while to comprehend what he was saying. He meant burn down the big house.

I stared back at him, trying to comprehend this dark proposal. Finally, I stammered out, "Good lord, Slim. *No*."

I went home that night chilled to the bone. It wasn't surprising to me, really, that Ronnie could be vengeful. In our barbershop talks, his cynicism had often bled over into vindictiveness. But I'd never heard him suggest anything so evil, and my response to him had been weak. I'd been too shocked to be emphatic enough.

Now I wondered: What has he done in the past? What is he still capable of, even now, even when he's sick? For all I knew, he'd dial some arsonist thug over the hospital phone that night and put him on the road to Keswick.

I was back in Ronnie's room extra early the next morning.

"I couldn't sleep, worrying about what you said." I didn't even want to repeat it, it was so awful. "If anything happened to Mrs. McIntyre, I couldn't live with it. You're not gonna hurt them, are you? If anything happens, I'll know it was you, and I'll never forgive you."

"Oh, shit, calm down," he said, half laughing. "I was just running my mouth."

But then, in a sinister voice, he coolly stated something just as ominous. His eyes turned to slits, and he boasted, smugly villainous, "I've righted some wrongs." He'd gone to a coal mine and burned it up—or did he say he blew it up? Later, I couldn't remember which word he used. Either one shook me up.

He told me that years before, on Roanoke's Williamson Road in the days when young people cruised the strip in their cars on Friday nights and people milled in and out of bars and pool halls, Ronnie had spotted an Albemarle County man he'd once known. He'd had a run-in with the guy back in Keswick long ago. He beat the man up and left him for dead on the sidewalk.

"He didn't even know me," Ronnie said with a wicked sneer.

ONE AFTERNOON I was looking out the window of his hospital room. The office buildings of downtown Roanoke sat below. I seldom had time to regard my new home like this. It looked dear to me.

"I love this little old town. I feel so at home here," I said.

"You could own a piece of that, girl. You could *be* somebody."

He proceeded to go on a rant. I shouldn't be only a reporter. I should be running the newspaper. Or I should have learned to ride horses back in Keswick. I should have married one of those rich men. Then I'd be sitting pretty in one of those mansions. He was getting all worked up about my failings.

"No, no, no," I protested. "I don't want any of that."

"Ya meek!" he suddenly stormed, his eyes blazing into me. "Ya meek! Just like your daddy!"

Several times Ronnie had implied to me that Daddy was a wimp. Ronnie jeered, for example, at the image of Daddy giving up guns. Daddy had long kept a .22 rifle near the back door to kill rabid animals and chicken-throttling varmints, but that was his only firearm. He'd quit hunting long ago, and fishing too. He felt rotten causing a fish to struggle on a

line with a hook in its mouth. Daddy's decision to quit killing wasn't far from Ronnie's own turn away from slaughtering wildlife. In his last years in the woods, Ronnie told me himself, he shot far more pictures than animals.

But Ronnie embraced any evidence that Daddy was a weakling, a failure as a man. If Ronnie was ostracized by Mom because of the blood he shared with the man who impregnated her, he was turning that around. I was tainted by Daddy's blood. Ronnie didn't understand me or Daddy. I didn't want to live in a mansion. I didn't want to be an editor or a publisher. Those people sat at their desks all day. I wanted to be out talking with people. I wanted to hear their stories, just as I was hearing his. And goddamn it, I *was* somebody.

AFTER RONNIE HAD been in the hospital a little more than a week, it looked as if he might go home. He sat up in bed grinning. He pressured the doctors to hurry up and let him go. Then, all of a sudden, his airways began to close up again. Cursing his body, he pulled violently, self-contemptuously, on the skin of his nostrils, trying to get air. He burped loudly. White, dried spittle covered his lips. Then he vomited blood. "I hurt so bad," he said, squeezing my hand. Doctors ran to him. He had a stomach ulcer. The doctors were in a bind. They were desperate to lower his blood pressure and keep him from stroking out, so they kept shoveling drugs into him. His body couldn't take it.

As aides rolled him to the operating room, I kissed his forehead and his hand. My apprehensions about him melted away; maybe these were the last words I'd say to him. I told him I'd be there when he got back. As they wheeled him away, he rasped, "Bye, baby."

A few hours later, the surgeon came by to tell me the operation went well. All the new medications and the stress of being in the hospital had burst a long-brewing ulcer in Ronnie. The surgeon patched the internal sore. In the operating room, Ronnie's larynx had once again gone into spasms. They reinserted the endotracheal tube. Ronnie was back on a ventilator. I came home with the smell of urine and blood stalled in my sinuses and the dread of another long recovery ahead of me.

HE WAS ALLOWED no water, only three cups of ice a day. I gave it to him on pink sponge-tipped sticks he popped into his mouth and sucked dry in an instant. With his hand on my shoulder, I rested my cheek on it until he fell asleep. I breathed along with him and the ventilator, like a prayer. As he slept, he dropped his hands into his lap, where they twitched in the motions of cutting hair.

I told him I loved him, and he gave me the sweetest smile. At home I'd still smell him, and I'd move my hands like his. My psychotherapist warned that I was merging emotionally with Ronnie and had gone beyond anything Ronnie himself would wish for me. Sometimes Ronnie would seem to be asleep, but then I'd notice him watching me through the slits of his eyes. He was observing me through those thin slices of his wavering irises.

SOON HE WAS breathing on his own again. He was better but more ornery. He refused to let his nurse reinsert his urinary catheter. As proof that he was peeing normally and able to control his urine, he presented her with a pee jug of clear

water, cooler than body temperature—obviously from his water cup.

He believed lying in bed was weakening him, so he insisted on sitting in his chair all day. When the nurse's aides stood him up, I spotted the edema in his upper thighs and the imprint of the plastic chair on his butt. If he didn't move around more—bed to chair, chair to bed—he'd develop bedsores. He wouldn't hear it.

He raged against me. "Damn, woman. If I keep on lying in this bed, I'll never get out of here!" But as I wearily left his room one night, he pointed to himself, then to me, and squeezed two fingers together. Yes, we were a team, but we were a tense team.

IN RONNIE'S SECOND week in the hospital, Mom and Daddy joined Daddy's eldest brother, Albert, and his family at a reunion in Northern Virginia. I'd planned to go, but Ronnie needed me. Mom lied about my absence. She told her in-laws I was working on a newspaper story. As I watched Ronnie's unwillingness to listen to the doctors and to take loving care of himself, I blamed her. He should have learned self-compassion from her—well, if she had any for herself. He should have stayed in school so he'd understand basic biology. He should have developed more faith in people. He should have learned some manners.

When I made my post-supper visit to him late one night after writing a story on deadline, he greeted me with "Where the hell you been?" He could be brutish and very hardheaded.

It turned out that Ronnie's health insurance would pay only thirty dollars of daily hospital charges in the thousands

of dollars. His bill was at $20,000 and rising. A hospital social worker suggested to me that Ronnie go on disability, but I knew he wouldn't go through the long process of applying for it. I hadn't told him yet that scans had shown mysterious masses on his lung and on a kidney. He could be in the hospital for a very long time.

When doctors switched him to a trach with a valve that allowed him to speak more clearly, he borrowed my blusher mirror to see how to put his finger over it to talk. He studied his stubble and his hair standing straight up. "Slim," he growled, "you're in a hell of a shape." He wanted to go back to work and start paying off his medical debts.

To ease his worries a little, I got his keys out of the hospital safe and drove to the Vinton post office to pick up his mail. In his rooms, Maxine and I poked around and found checks so that he could pay some bills. Maxine was becoming my ally. I was calling her Max now, as Ronnie did. In Ronnie's rubble, I found twenty or more nose sprays—evidence of his long battle against the narrowing of his upper airways from acromegaly.

Mom was feeling guilty that she'd visited her brother-in-law while I was down in Roanoke looking after her sick son. She called me, wanting to come see Ronnie. She wanted to bake him a cake and send him flowers and gifts. I ran it all by Ronnie. Just the thought of her and Daddy coming back to stare at him again alarmed Ronnie and probably spiked his blood pressure. Please, he begged, don't let them come. Tell them he'd be glad to see them later on, which was probably a lie. But no, not right now. *Please.*

Mom was incensed. "I see what's going on," she snarled at me over the phone, insinuating that Ronnie was trying to

turn me against her. She went on, her hard jaw audible: "Well, I don't want to hear any crap about how Adria was down in Roanoke and didn't go see Ronnie. Everything I've offered to do wasn't wanted." In her eyes, he was bad. "Someday," she warned me, "you will see it." Where was my charitable mother, the compassionate one I knew so well? She vanished whenever Ronnie appeared.

She and Daddy drove to Roanoke and stayed with me the next night. As payback for my watching over Ronnie, they helped me trim shrubbery and weed flower beds. Daddy was down on his knees in my privet hedges, pulling out poison ivy. In the living room, I was trying to get Mom to talk about Ronnie.

"It's gotta be hard," I said gingerly. "All those years you kept him a secret. Makes sense you're still conflicted about him."

She snapped back, "You don't know how I feel." We returned to yard work.

Trying to Help

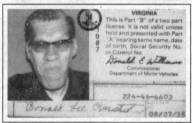

Early in Ronnie's fourth week in the hospital, he awoke in tip-top form. He was almost jolly. He licked his breakfast plate clean. By lunchtime, though, he'd transformed into a weak, ghostly-white figure. He fainted on his bedside potty. The chief resident quickly determined that Ronnie was losing blood from his small intestine.

Ronnie grabbed the nurses' hands. "Help me!" He thought he was bleeding to death. He rushed them to transfer him to the gurney and whisk him to the OR. It had been only two weeks since his last surgery. Once again, I watched as they wheeled him away. Once again, I didn't know if I'd see him again.

From a pay phone, I called Mom to let her know he was headed back to surgery. Cheery "uh-huhs" were her odd response. A neighbor lady was visiting. Mom kept a smile in her voice as, on the other end, I described the grim scene at Community Hospital. Mom didn't want to signal that anything was wrong. She didn't want her friend to know she had a son fighting for his life down in Roanoke, or that she had a son at all.

My therapist believed Mom was incapable of seeing Ronnie as a valuable person. That's why she responded with coldness to my reports of his difficulties. If she were to believe that Ronnie was a worthy individual, she'd have to face a lifetime of her errors concerning him. So it was easier for her to consider him of marginal importance.

As before, doctors had been throwing medications at Ronnie's matrix of maladies, doing their best to help him. His body still couldn't tolerate all the drugs. This time, apparently, an anticoagulant set off the blood loss. His gut was a mess. The surgeon went in and vacuumed out great globs of clotted blood. Once again, nurses began pumping blood and plasma back into Ronnie.

He went days without eating. He'd lie in bed and imagine the aisles of his Vinton supermarket. "Oh, Kroger," he said dreamily. "Melons, cheese, peanut butter . . ." He was mastering his new talking trach, so we were conversing again. He was looking forward to dipping a slice of deep-dish pepperoni into the Italian dressing of a tossed salad at his favorite pizzeria.

I was back at the newspaper but coming by to see him before work, at lunch, and at night. I was keeping up with the doctors' medical strategies and trying to learn about disability and Medicaid in hopes I could talk Ronnie into applying

for them. His hospital bill was at about $60,000 already, three times the amount he had in savings. When I wasn't thinking about his financial fix, I was still assimilating this awful family history. Plus, I was trying to get some sleep, some exercise, some peace while calling Mom and Max two or three times a day with updates.

Meanwhile, Ronnie's doctors were talking with him more urgently now about lining up pituitary surgery at the University of Virginia Medical Center. A specialist there was eager to get that tumor out. Ronnie said he'd rather die from his disease. He thundered to his doctors, his big hands splayed out in front of him, "Put on the top of the ledger: 'He is going back to work!' I want OUT of here!"

What I was imagining was far worse than Ronnie's vision of a quick death. Acromegaly could blind him, cause a stroke, and land him in a nursing home, which would be far more torturous than a hospital. A nursing home would spell the end for Ronnie.

I was growing more impatient by the day with his simplistic views. He thought he could pay a few dollars a month on his medical debts, but the figures he was imagining—ten dollars a month, twenty, twenty-five dollars tops—wouldn't be enough for his surgeon, anesthesiologist, pulmonologist, radiologist, internist, pathologist, laboratories, or for the hospital itself. Even if they agreed to such tiny outlays, would Ronnie be able to remember payments on a dozen bills each month? He was disorganized. He'd lived an old-fashioned life. He'd been able to walk or drive to his creditors and plop down cash. He rarely wrote checks or mailed them. I offered to help with his debts. I could afford $200 a month.

As Mother's Day approached, I toyed with the idea of send-

ing Mom a card "from both of us," which would have been cruel. In her mind, Ronnie and I were not really connected. Instead, I mailed a card "from your daughter." She was so distrustful of Ronnie that I had recently asked what awful things had he done. Had he exposed himself as a boy? "No." Then, "Well, what did he do?" Rape somebody? Injure somebody? "No," she said, annoyed. "He just stole things, Mary Carter." She didn't tell me he'd threatened to kill her.

A MONTH AFTER he arrived at the hospital, Ronnie was out of the ICU and in a regular hospital room. They'd removed his urinary catheter and taken the pesky oxygen cannula out of his nose. He was attached now only to intravenous bags of fluids and to antibiotics. Now that he was out of the woods, I was letting go of some of my watchful edge, and my adrenaline was on the wane. I nearly passed out as I walked back to work after a lunchtime visit. For the first time, Ronnie called me at home that night to make sure I was okay.

He was back in physical therapy and on the road toward home. I was cutting back to two visits a day. Shortly before he moved from the ICU to a regular room, a nurse looked at him and his bags of belongings sitting there, ready to go, and commented that he looked like an orphan. I wondered if he caught that.

Max had been in to see him. He promised her that he wouldn't be so grumpy anymore. He was going to be nice.

MAY WAS MY favorite month. I'd spent most of it in the hospital with Ronnie. The tight fern fronds, the purple wild violets,

the broad-and-glossy-leafed wildflower called mayapple—I'd failed to even notice them in the lowland Roanoke Valley that year. They'd matured into their thick, dusty summer incarnations by the time Ronnie was better.

I dialed back the season and found the freshness of early May again in a one-night stay at Mountain Lake, a lodge an hour west and four thousand feet of elevation away from home. Ronnie had taken his girlfriends there in the old days. Tender celery-green leaves were just popping out on the trees. The hotel, set within a nature preserve, allowed trees to fall undisturbed in the woods and be shrouded with moss and lichens. I tromped through the woods with the chipmunks and heard birdsong that was new to me. Even Ronnie was glad to see me get away. "You've got a life too," I was surprised to hear him say.

ON MAY 25, after thirty-nine days in the hospital, Ronnie's hour of release was set for 11:00 a.m. As he awaited his discharge, he was giddy as a kid heading to Disney World. "Eleven o'clock," he intoned, watching the second hand creep toward the hour on his wall clock. "Let the sun shine on this poor old country boy one more time."

I pulled my Honda Civic hatchback around to the hospital entrance. Ronnie scrunched down to fit into the squat car. When we pulled up to Max's house, his weakness suddenly made itself known. Walking thirty feet from the car to the front porch was the most work Ronnie had done in almost two months. The rubber tips of his crutches dragged with each step.

Dear, chipper Max stood on the front porch waiting for

us. We settled Ronnie into a chair out there and went upstairs to case out his room. My heart sank as Max pulled back the blankets on his bed. His only sheet, a fitted bottom one, was the color of long-steeped tea. It hadn't been changed in years, maybe never.

He lacked the strength to make it up the stairs. Max brought him a pillow and a blanket so he could sleep downstairs on the couch that Friday night. When I drove up the next morning, Max was out in the sunny backyard, cheerfully hanging Ronnie's pillows and blankets on the clothesline. She'd thrown out the sheet. Upstairs, she'd been wrestling to pin a clean white cloth onto Ronnie's filthy mattress.

I'd foolishly thought that once Ronnie was home, everything would get easier. But he was an invalid. He was a terminally ill man recovering from two GI tract surgeries. An army of doctors, nurses, aides, physical therapists, and dietitians had tended to him for five weeks. He'd gotten used to that level of care.

Max was seventy-one years old. How much should she be expected to do for Ronnie? I still wasn't sure how close the two of them really were, or how natural it would be for her to look after him. All the daily services of the hospital suddenly popped into my mind—the baths, the meals, the carefully organized prescriptions, the clean sheets, the towels, the adjustable bed. We had none of that.

I left the two of them that Saturday afternoon to go to a festival with a friend. The next morning, Max's sister, Thelma, called, extremely upset. Ronnie had told me about Thelma. He called her Delma because his thick tongue couldn't position itself for *th* sounds. Thelma thought Max had suffered a ministroke sometime after I'd left on Saturday. When Thelma

called the house that evening, Max sounded confused and momentarily wasn't even aware that Ronnie was back home. Thelma rushed there and spotted a bruise on Max's forehead. She thought Max had fallen.

I went straight over. Max looked okay, but I needed to go to the store for her and to help out however I could. I called one of Ronnie's doctors and explained that Ronnie's house-mate wasn't up to caring for him. A home nurse was sched-uled to start coming twice a week soon; the doctor would try to make that a daily service.

Ronnie and I went over his medical bills at the dining room table that evening. He had trouble comprehending the paper-work. He was grouchy, impatient. He couldn't concentrate. He was annoyed with everything. I'd bought butter when he wanted margarine. I'd bought store-brand cheddar when he wanted fontina. "Hell, woman, I may be a hillbilly, but I'm a hillbilly who peeked over the fence."

That night, Max and I helped him up the stairs, through his door, and by the piles of stinking shoes to his clean bed. Once we got him there, Max hurried off toward her room.

"I don't mean to be cross with you, baby," Ronnie told me.

"I know, I know."

"It's just that I get so flustrated. I'm just scared to death.

"Hey, Max," Ronnie hollered down the hall. "Get on back in here."

Sitting on the edge of his bed, he took our hands and looked up at us tenderly. "A man shouldn't fuss at the only two bud-dies he's got. I love you two." He squeezed our hands, and he hugged Max. She told me later it was the first time he'd ever hugged her.

RONNIE, MAX, AND I watched that summer go by in warm
evenings on their front porch. Max kicked her short legs up
and down from her tall chair like a little girl. She asked me
to tell her stories about the places I'd been and the people I'd
met. I dusted off my travels around Europe and my long ram-
ble around Colorado from a few years earlier. I entertained
her with verbal travelogues about small Virginia towns she'd
never seen, just a few hours from her house. Meanwhile, my
separate life of friends, mountain hikes, parties, dancing, and
quiet evenings on my own front porch was slipping away
again. I was into my seventh intense week of one-on-one
with Ronnie. That weekend, Max and I crawled inside his old
cars, his 1974 Mercury Marquis Brougham sedan and his 1978
Dodge Ramcharger sport utility vehicle, to replace his out-
dated county decals.

I bought him an electric shaver. Otherwise I'd have to use
an old-style bladed razor on those precipitous facial features
and baggy skin. I bathed the upper half of him. As the wash-
cloth slid over his face, the acute ridges of those overgrown
bones jolted me—such great cliffs and crags on one long face.
I hoped he didn't catch the momentary hesitation of my fin-
gers as they encountered the bones' sharp edges through the
warm, soapy cloth. I imagined his bones being dug up one day
and somebody asking, *What kind of man was this?*

I WAS GETTING no exercise. I was putting on weight. Ev-
ery time I was at their house, however, Ronnie and Max were
ordering me, "Eat!" I'd go to the store for cherry-vanilla ice
cream for them. "Eat!" he'd bellow. I'd bring them greasy
fried fish from Libby Hill Seafood. "Eat!" I wanted to get

in shape again and maybe meet a man. "If she meets a man," Ronnie said, sotto voce, to Max, "she won't have so much time for me."

One night Ronnie, Max, and I were watching *CBS Evening News* when a foreign correspondent appeared on-screen. He'd been a classmate of mine at Columbia. Ronnie didn't even know I'd gone to Columbia. He didn't know that I'd earned a master's degree there or that I'd ever lived in New York. When he visited the folks in the old days, they didn't mention me, and he didn't dare ask.

As I left that Sunday night, Ronnie proclaimed that getting sick had changed his life in a good way. Before, he asserted, somewhat emotionally, "I was scared of people." He wouldn't have much to do with them. I replied, "Well, maybe you thought they'd let you down." He winked at me and nodded.

Ronnie and I spent Memorial Day at his house. Max and Thelma were with their mother in the country. We rambled around throughout the big, airy house the Booth family had built in the thirties. Every few feet Ronnie leaned on his crutches and told me a story. At a living room window, he spotted a detail that made him chuckle. Years before, a squirrel came down the chimney, and before Ronnie and Max knew that it was inside, it gnawed on a windowsill trying to get out. Its tooth marks, now painted over, were still there.

Ronnie captured the squirrel in a humane trap. At first he was going to shoot it. But then he'd have to fire into the metal trap, and that would mangle it. "I thought, well, I'll knife the son of a bitch. But he'd bleed all over the goddamned place. I thought, maybe I'll drown you. But I don't have the heart for that."

The squirrel was shivering in the trap. "That could have

been me," remembered Ronnie, so often an unwanted intruder himself. So he put newspaper under the trap and took the squirrel to his car. "Come on," he told it. "We're going to take a little drive." Ronnie found a deserted mansion out in the country, with a big yard and plenty of oaks and other nut trees. He opened the trap and out popped the squirrel. It peed on the tip of his shoe, chirped twice, and headed straight for the oaks. Ronnie thought to himself, *Well, maybe I did something that day.* He told me he tried not to bully people or any creatures, at least not those less powerful than him. He knew how they felt. A primitive gospel, Ronnie-style, all decked out with "goddamns" and "sons-a-bitches."

EVERY DAY AT my newsroom desk, I was calling Ronnie's creditors to explain that he couldn't pay his bills in full but that he was working on them. Then I'd go see him after work, and he'd bark orders at me. I took him takeout dinners from the Kroger deli and chain restaurants. Lots of mac 'n cheese, coleslaw, and fried fish. As we ate at Maxine's dining room table, if Ronnie wanted more of a dish, he wouldn't ask me to hand it to him. He'd point to it and grunt. What did I expect? He hadn't really been part of a family since he left Polly and Roy's house at age six. How could he know how to conduct himself at a meal?

A friend of mine reminded me how different Ronnie and I were—in life experience, in education, in social class, in every way. I'd imagined him becoming my congenial dinner companion. That wasn't going to happen. He was a lip-smacking diner, a rude, roaring, cursing giant.

Even with his new electric razor, Ronnie wouldn't shave

himself; he waited for me to come over and do it. Many days
he was nothing but a bullheaded weight on me. Max, mean-
while, denied him nothing. She served up meals of a dozen
dishes. She even cleaned out his scummy refrigerator.

HIS SIXTH DAY home, I took a break. Ronnie was blue all
day. He sat on the porch and watched for my Honda. Late in
the day, he told Max, "I don't guess Mary Carter's coming."
I was sorry about that, but I needed to do my own laundry,
mow my own yard, and dump weeks' worth of garbage on my
compost pile.

The hospital was asking Ronnie for one hundred dollars a
month on his bill of $72,541. If he agreed, the hospital would
drag its feet going after his savings. That was generous. But to
Ronnie, who charged only up to five dollars a haircut, a hun-
dred bucks was a king's ransom. He'd pay twenty-five dollars
and not a penny more. Then there were the ten or more other
doctors and companies demanding payment. All told at that
point, he owed upwards of $84,000. I located a lawyer who spe-
cialized in medical indebtedness. Ronnie refused to see her.

"Where you been?" he'd greet me when I arrived at the
house, time after time. "Get me some Kleenex! Go get me some
sinus medicine!" I asked him to soften his machine-gun orders,
but I knew he only did it because he was scared. He was sorry
he ordered me around. "I miss you when you're not here," he
said. Every time I'd leave, he'd sadly say, "I hate to see you go."

What was I going to do? I'd created all these expectations.
But could I keep this up? I was already dreading each arrival
at his house and his daily demands. But Maxine shouldn't be
burdened with them. Should I?

THELMA TOOK MAX on another day trip. Max left the fridge loaded with food and instructed Ronnie to eat it before it went bad. He was wasting food. Still, Ronnie pined for a fresh tub of Kentucky Fried Chicken, so I went to the nearest KFC. "You better take the leftovers home, or Max will give me hell for buying more."

A bit later, Maxine walked in and caught us, mid-chicken. We looked sheepish, and we all laughed. She knew Ronnie was making up for weeks of misery. Maybe years of it. He was slowly becoming a useful member of her household again. That morning, near the back door, he'd killed a black snake with his crutch.

THAT JUNE OF 1990, Ronnie was still refusing surgery. He had some rat poison up in his room. If he lost his sight, he'd poison himself, he said. I let that pass for now and focused on our good times together. "Bring some pictures of Bridlespur," he asked, "so Max can see what it looks like."

I dug out a little album of photos Mom had put together for my last birthday. Mom, Daddy, the granddaddies. Mary Carter at three in front of our house. Mary Carter on the first day of school. Ronnie in the back in a group shot, towering over me and a bunch of other little kids. Ronnie grinned affectionately at the pictures. I might still be absorbing the fact of his exclusion, but it was old news to him. Right then, right there, with my head nudging Ronnie's and Max's as they viewed the little book, I knew that though he envied me, he also loved me.

I CALLED A pituitary specialist who'd offered to help Ronnie and told her I hadn't been able to talk him into surgery. She warned that he might already have lost vision. He might be keeping it to himself. I needed to get him to the University of Virginia Medical Center as soon as possible. I knew his bad hip and long legs would be cramped in my small car for the two-hour ride. I looked into renting a bigger car. Still, Ronnie wouldn't go.

His airways were giving him fits. When his right nostril clamped shut, he wanted to take a knife and cut it open. His self-contempt was horrifying. Whenever he couldn't recall a word, he'd curse himself and clobber whatever furniture he was near. "You big, old, ignorant hillbilly." He often pointed an imaginary gun to his head and pulled the trigger.

IT WAS TIME for Ronnie's talking trach to be removed, and he asked me to take him to the ear, nose, and throat specialist in downtown Roanoke. He'd been in Vinton thirty years, and Roanoke, not exactly a metropolis, had come to seem like one to Ronnie. He feared he'd have trouble finding a parking space.

In the waiting room, a young boy's bored, restless eyes landed on Ronnie. The kid silently snickered. Ronnie lowered his giant head into his chest and kept his eyes down. Seeing that the boy's father wasn't going to stop the kid, Ronnie limped around the corner and waited in the hall by the elevator, and I followed. I watched this silent drama but didn't say anything. That would have made it worse for Ronnie. In-

stead, I stared at the boy, still leering from the doorway, and I wouldn't quit. It took him a while to notice me, and when he did, I wordlessly drilled every bit of my fury into his eyeballs and wouldn't let up. Time after time he'd look away, then look back at me. *See? See how it feels?* He stopped looking.

WITH RONNIE STILL denying he had acromegaly, I tried another tack. I brought a medical textbook with pictures of other men with the disease. If he saw the similarities between him and them, maybe he'd accept his diagnosis. But he couldn't see what they had in common. Through one of his doctors, I contacted a local man around Ronnie's age who had acromegaly and had recovered from tumor removal. The man and his wife, middle-aged like Ronnie and extremely friendly, came by to see Ronnie. He barely listened to their story of how much better the man felt.

No, Ronnie told me after they'd gone, doctors were just trying to trap him. They wanted to keep him from going back to the barbershop. Maybe Ronnie was nuts after all. Why would anybody not move to prevent blindness and death? Pale, thin, coughing, he looked dreadful. Bloody mucus gathered at the scab where his trach had been. I warned him that rat poison probably wouldn't kill him. It would just tear up his gut and send him back to the OR. He wouldn't budge. "No, it's cyanide. It'll work."

Ronnie was sophisticated about a few things—Virginia history, wild turkeys, barbering, the culture and geology of the central Appalachians. But when it came to physiology and finances and medical bureaucracies and human relations, he was in the dark. Education at its best illumines all the workings of

humanity. Ronnie, a recluse, had only seen a sliver's glimpse of them. "Good night, Mr. O.," I called out as I left that evening. "O for obstinate."

BY JULY, ALMOST six weeks after Ronnie returned home, he and Max were quarreling. She called me very upset on a Saturday. His food hoarding had overstuffed her fridge. Before, they'd lived fairly independent lives. Now he was demanding that she cook him big meals. That day, she'd helped him don elasticized socks to reduce blood clots. It took serious muscle to pull those stockings on. I'd had trouble doing it for him, and I was a foot taller and thirty years younger than Max. As she struggled, Ronnie cursed her. She slammed his bedroom door behind her and refused to do any more. I went right over.

I stuffed him into my car and drove him over to see my house, across the valley from Vinton. Up my front walk, Ronnie hauled his crutches along but didn't use them. He held them flaring out from under each arm, like some giant-winged, bony bird galumphing along, hunched forward to compensate for his bad right hip and leg. He looked up admiringly at my 1920s brick Tudor, with Boston ivy climbing up its front.

He sat in my kitchen nook and gazed contentedly out the bay window at my charming old brick garage and my wooded backyard. He petted my cats, Virginia and Rural Earl. I showed him around the upstairs and the attic room where I watched TV. He seemed to get a kick out of seeing where I lived. He called my Tudor a "two door," as though it were a sedan.

That summer, I drove him along the Blue Ridge Parkway. We cruised slowly by grazing cows, old barns, and split-rail

fences. We stopped at overlooks and glanced way off at West
Virginia's Allegheny Mountains, where Ronnie had once ex-
plored so freely. In my car, at home, even at work, I smelled
Ronnie. I smelled his bitterness on my own skin. I tried to
scrub it off. I changed shampoos. I tried cologne, deodorant,
and perfumed body lotion. I dumped carpet-cleaning powder
on my car seats. The acrid smell of him remained. I was hav-
ing trouble with my blood tie to my sick, deeply embittered
brother. Smelling like him seemed awfully close to being him.

MY INCLINATION WAS always to write about poor people; all
my favorite stories were about them. Ronnie and Max reveled
in my newspaper tales and agreed that I was a modern-day
Mary Worth, a sob-sister comic strip character wrapped up in
other people's problems. I found poor people generally more
interesting than better-off people. They often were wiser and
more compassionate. They had a handle on how power ele-
vates some and squashes others. But confronting deprivation
and the lack of education in my own brother, being around
the results of his alienation and his poverty of spirit every day,
was impoverishing me. I wanted to rise above my aversion to
him, but he was dragging me down. He was keeping me from
my healthy life. And yet I couldn't pull myself away.

I was his audience. We all long for someone to sit and listen
to the stories of our pasts. Ronnie believed I was the one to
do that for him. He was his customers' ear; I was his. He was
sucking me dry, and I was weary of him portraying every-
body as a son of a bitch. He saw selfish motives everywhere.
Susan, his caring, conscientious home health nurse, drove to
the pharmacy for one of his prescriptions, but Ronnie didn't

appreciate it. She was just a drone, a "dumb broad," he grumbled to me. His young doctor, Will Truslow, spent one of his rare free hours driving across the valley to check on Ronnie, yet Ronnie didn't recognize his visit as an act of benevolence. Ronnie didn't seem to believe people did things out of kindness. It hadn't happened much to him.

BACK AT THE hospital, I'd encouraged his talk of us traveling together up in the mountains. Now, when he proposed doing just that, I froze and didn't say anything. I felt ungenerous, but the thought of being stuck alone with him in the wilderness filled me with dread. I felt I should be trying to help my brother have whatever fun he could, but he was a burden. Now I doubted I'd ever write about him. I'd have to confess to all this, and I was too ashamed.

He saved me from the mountain camping trips because in late July, after he'd been home two months, Ronnie began to smile again. He'd just reopened the barbershop.

Losses, Gains, Losses

The last driver's license photo taken of Ronnie, a
few weeks before his death.

With late summer's undulating cicada buzz screeching
in our ears, Ronnie, Max, and I returned to something like our usual lives. Each of us basked in our reclaimed
freedoms. Once again, unrealistically and for my own selfish
reasons, I fantasized that Ronnie was going to be all right.

He was in the best spirits I'd ever seen when I took a New
York friend by the shop to meet him. For a kid's buzz cut,
Ronnie covered the top of the boy's head with his hand and
twisted it as surely as the lid on a pickle jar brimming with
juice. My friend ran a Southern-flavored club in Chelsea.
Ronnie was captivated by stories of Mick Jagger and Bruce
Springsteen dropping by to see new acts. Ronnie'd always

wanted to see Manhattan. He'd heard there was a store there with an entire floor of candy.

On August 27, a Monday, Ronnie was turning fifty-five. Max and I excitedly cooked up plans for a surprise party. I had to be in Richmond for a story that day, so we'd have the party the next day. That way, Ronnie would be even more surprised. I'd get the cake; Max, the ice cream. I invited Thelma, who lived across the valley, and six other members of the Booth family from neighboring houses along Halliahurst Avenue.

Tuesday morning, I bought the cake, birthday plates, and napkins. I called Max but got no answer. *She must be out buying the ice cream.* Ronnie, unaware of the party, asked me to pick him up at the barbershop at five o'clock to try out a new pizza place as a birthday celebration. Midafternoon, I went by Max's. No answer at the door. I was sleepy from long workdays, so I curled up on the porch in a yellow secondhand recliner Max bought for Ronnie while he was in the hospital. Her car was in the driveway. *She must be down the street.*

Alpha, Max's cousin next door, had been trying for hours to reach Max. She'd called Thelma, who didn't know where she was. Alpha brought a house key and disappeared inside. In a bit, she called down, alarmed. "Mary, come here! Quick!" Max, in a blue nightgown and nylon sleeping cap, was on her stomach in bed, her face mashed into her pillow. Her right foot was turning blue. I clapped my hands and shouted, "Max! Max!" No response.

Alpha dialed the rescue squad. We decided not to turn Max over. The next twenty minutes were a blur of medics, a gurney, family members, phone calls. That sinking body lacked every measure of the girlish, joyful Max. She was dead, of a stroke.

At the barbershop, Ronnie was in his barber's chair reading one of his wrecked-car magazines. Days before, he'd been dreaming of us driving together to South Dakota to buy him one of those hot deals out in the Badlands. I was supposed to ride shotgun. I stepped in the door and sat down. "Slim, I got some bad news." He looked up and waited. He wasn't expecting anything this bad, but I went on, "Max is dead."

We sat nearly three hours as he absorbed it. "Well," he finally said, solemnly, "I probably just lost the best friend I ever had." She'd even offered to pay for his pituitary surgery. When he went home that night, he found clues that she'd tried to start her day. A cereal bowl he'd left in the sink before heading to work had been washed. The toilet seat upstairs was down. He thought she must have felt bad, so she crawled back into bed.

We went together to the night-before-the-funeral visitation at a Vinton funeral home. Then we sat on the porch at Max's and talked about her. Four months earlier, after the Vinton medics raced Ronnie to the hospital, Max sent them a note of thanks and a hundred-dollar donation. I recalled her remorse when she accidentally stepped on an ant. I'd known Max only a few months, and I missed her already.

She'd told Ronnie many times that she'd named him as the beneficiary of a $100,000 life insurance policy and that her will would state that he could live out his days in her house. We went together to her funeral. He sent a dozen red roses, her favorites. He wore his best shirt and tie, and because it was a hot August day, he carried his classiest sport coat, a tan suede, on his arm.

That September, between out-of-town newspaper assignments, I dropped by the shop. He rehashed friends' promises

of long ago, and not just Max's. A customer had vowed to be-
queath his Land Rover to Ronnie, who loved to fancy himself a
dude with money and a jazzy car. I figured these promises were
mere mentions that grew in Ronnie's imagination and were
quickly forgotten by the speakers. But Ronnie was counting on
these pledges. They gave him things to look forward to.

Thelma was already saying Max had left no will, so the
lifetime home was out, though he could stay indefinitely.
Ronnie was still counting on the life insurance. He said Max
had taken out a policy for the same amount for Thelma. He'd
seen the paperwork for his policy, with his name and Social
Security number on it.

But where would he live? Max's survivors would even-
tually sell the house. They had comfortable homes already
and were too old to move. How could this sick man, this re-
sister of change, so burdened with medical debts, cope with
the nineties economy? Other than modest bills incurred at
his barbershop, he hadn't paid rent or utilities for years, and
back when he rented his rooms, they were only ten bucks
a week. Even in low-cost Vinton, the tiniest studio apart-
ment would go for at least $300 a month. Ronnie insisted he
couldn't afford that.

He was nervous in the house at night. He'd heard some-
thing one evening just before I called. He poked a loaded
shotgun out the front door. Young kids were carrying on in
the street. Alpha's daughter, next door, kept bringing home-
cooked meals over and letting herself in with a key. Ronnie's
anxiety and stockpile of weapons led me to imagine tragic
scenarios.

Soon Ronnie hinted he wanted to move in with me. He said
it twice. If the Booths tossed him out, he'd come knocking on

my door and ask to rent my attic room. I tried to imagine my quiet, solitary house, my sanctuary from work and stress—my refuge from *Ronnie*—with him living in it. He'd be thundering around upstairs. We'd be sharing my one and only bathroom. I'd just hosted a Dutch journalist for five days while he was working in our part of Virginia. Even that guy violated my sense of peace and retreat, and he was low-key and undemanding. I didn't respond to Ronnie. I did say that I'd help him find an apartment and that I'd help him pay for it.

I'd won a fellowship for eugenics research at a Charlottesville humanities center for the following spring semester. If Ronnie moved into my house, I wouldn't be there to look after him. Could I count on him to make the right judgments on sick cats, nosy neighbors, and home maintenance? I'd planned to come home on weekends to decompress. With Ronnie there, he'd command those days, and it wouldn't be my house anymore. Mom said it would kill her if he moved in. She'd feel as though she'd ruined my life. "Mary Carter, don't let him do it." I heard agitation, fear, and regret in her voice. Her first kid had been nothing but trouble, and now he was threatening her favorite one.

EARLY THAT OCTOBER, while I was at work, Ronnie drove himself to a checkup with Will Truslow, the young doctor who'd made the house call over the summer. Ronnie's blood pressure was 240/150. Will wanted to put him in the hospital. Ronnie refused, so nurses fed him pills all afternoon to get the pressure down before letting him return to his shop. Will called to let me know.

I rushed to the barbershop. Ronnie was reading another

issue of *Wheels and Deals* and obsessing about the money coming his way. Any fixation like this would consume his every waking hour. What was taking so long with his goddamned windfall? He rolled up the car magazine and angrily whapped it on his leg, then the barber chair, then the palm of his other hand. *Whap! Whap! Whap!*

His latest idea was to buy a trailer near Vinton. Thank God he'd decided my house was too far a drive from the barbershop. When I'd see him that fall, he'd be lighthearted sometimes, morose others. When I was home from trips out of town, I'd go over and describe my experiences, such as a visit to New York to see that Chelsea nightclub. Ronnie tried to comprehend New York as I talked about the skyscrapers and the fact that even at three o'clock in the morning, the low muffled roar of trucks, trains, planes, and heating systems never ceased. When Ronnie took on something beyond his imagining, the skin crawled slowly over his giant frowning brow. He was one man whose thinking was actually visible.

I dropped by the house another time after work in late October. His cars were out back, so I thought he must be home. He didn't come to the door. I went to a house down the street and called. No answer. I got nervous. It was looking like a replay of the day Max died, so I ran for Alpha and the house key. Just as she was unlocking the door, Ronnie appeared and let us in.

Nighttime temperatures were at freezing, but Ronnie hadn't turned on the furnace—because Thelma hadn't called to give him permission. He was running two kerosene heaters and contemplating a third. Alpha and I warned him about the dangers of that and urged him to turn on the central heat. Surely Thelma assumed he would. She wouldn't think it necessary to tell him. He didn't even feel entitled to warmth.

I rode with him in his Ramcharger for a takeout fish dinner. From the back seat I watched him crawl through the passenger door, get settled behind the wheel, and drag his bad right leg, about four feet long, across the front seat. It was easier for him to get in the car that way.

He returned a hunting film to a video store and laughed at how the young guy there was always pitching what Ronnie called screw movies. Ronnie wasn't interested in sex anymore. He thought it was due to his age. The acromegaly literature listed loss of libido as one of the most common symptoms.

Parked in back of the house as he gobbled his flounder and french fries, Ronnie told me he was keeping the barbershop open later. He was putting in extra hours to pay his medical bills. He belched loudly and guzzled a bottle of Mylanta between bites of fish. He pulled on his nostrils. He cracked his knuckles, first finger by finger, then all his fingers bent back in a chorus of popping joints. Acromegaly caused every one of those behaviors.

Mom and Daddy were coming for Thanksgiving lunch and wanted to see him too. No, he said. Once again, he mentioned burning down the big house at Bridlespur, and once again, I said it would break my heart.

HE WAS IN surprisingly good spirits when I'd go by the barbershop that fall. I'd listen to his colorful language—cars were "chines," pronounced "sheens." I wished like hell I could record him, but he wouldn't allow it. What a writer Ronnie might have been. His language was blunt, economical, Dashiell Hammett–like. No waste, no fat from those fat lips.

At Thanksgiving, I told Mom I wished she'd apologize

to Ronnie. "Apologize for what?" she snarled. "Just tell him
you're sorry his life turned out to be so hard." She rolled her
eyes. She had always had trouble with apologies. I'd never
heard her deliver a sincere one to me or to anybody, even when
she was clearly in the wrong. Instead, she'd spit out, "Well,
I'm sorry," in an angry, defensive tone. That would hurt Ron-
nie all the more. After my folks left, I drove over. He was on
the porch speaking again of suicide.

Thelma had just told him that Max had changed her bene-
ficiaries a few days before her death. Max's brother would re-
ceive the insurance money earmarked for Ronnie. Years later,
Thelma's boyfriend, a trustworthy source in my newspaper
work, confirmed that after Ronnie cursed Max that summer,
Max had indeed taken his name off the policy. It was probably
when he cursed her because she couldn't pull those support
hose over his big feet.

I drove Ronnie around the valley, along the Roanoke River,
and all around, trying to get his mind off his disappointments.
He was lower than ever, and when he was low, he was hateful.
As we rode through a park, he said he used to walk there until
"the coons" started dealing drugs there. I dropped him off at
his house just before bedtime. "I'll sit here 'til you get inside.
In case somebody pops you in the head."

"Naw," he said wearily, wrestling his long legs out the car
door. "Nobody's gonna get me. Nobody wants me." Of all
the painful things he ever said, that is the one that replays in
my head all these years since. Nobody did want Ronnie. I was
trying to. But it was hard.

FOR WEEKS HE brooded over what he saw as Max's betrayal. She could have at least left him one of her little rental houses. Her reneging on her promise, he told me, made him understand why people kill in anger. "Like maybe the criminal isn't so bad after all."

I invited him out to see *Dances with Wolves*. Western history, American Indians, settlers—of all the movies from that era, this was the one for him. No, he needed to go home and keep the water pipes from freezing. "Or they'll kick my ass out."

SOON MY FOLKS were near Vinton for a cousin's funeral. After, they went by the shop to invite Ronnie to lunch. The shop door was locked. Ronnie usually latched it at lunchtime, even if he remained inside. Through the plate glass of the door and in the mirror behind Ronnie, they watched him in the barber chair, holding up a newspaper that shielded his face from theirs. "Ronnie? *Ronnie!*" Mom called out. "Please, Ronnie. We just want to see you." She tapped her lipstick tube on the glass. He never lowered the paper. They gave up and drove away.

THAT CHRISTMAS OF 1990, Ronnie had rarely been so gloomy. He was belching furiously. He cursed everybody. He rammed his finger into a waxy ear and lamented to me the long list of wrongs committed against him. He smelled as if he hadn't showered in many days. I now linked our common odor to our sad, sour mother.

He was angriest with doctors. An anesthesiologist had sent a bill for $800. "Right at Christmas," Ronnie said indignantly. His doctors were hanging out in their fine offices over there in Roanoke, chortling over how they were fleecing poor old Ronnie Overstreet. He was even mad at the women who ran the home-cooking place around the corner from his shop that had been his lunch place for decades. He was sure it was their fried chow that upset his gut. The female cooks and waitresses were trying to distract him from their greasy food with their tight pants and "big titties."

Why did I keep thinking I was going to make Ronnie a cheerful, unwounded, trusting soul? I couldn't do that if I quit my job, emptied my savings, and devoted the rest of my life to it. I was too late. I was dealing with a rupture more than a half century old and with an illness whose head-to-toe disruptions hurt him thoroughly and confounded his simple understanding of the body's workings. I wanted to ask if I could write about him eventually, but I knew he would turn the idea over in his mind a thousand times, and it would just be another stressor. Did I have the right to tell his story? I'm still not sure.

THAT CHRISTMAS, PEOPLE were fixated by my stories about a baby found barely alive in a dumpster near downtown Roanoke. On December 19, an unemployed construction worker digging for aluminum cans heard what he thought was a sick cat or a crying doll. He upended a plastic garbage bag and out slid a cardboard box containing a fully developed newborn boy, six pounds, eight ounces, wrapped in a yellow-flowered blanket.

The baby suffered cardiovascular collapse and brain damage from exposure to overnight temperatures in the forties. Named Isaiah by intensive care nurses, he died on Christmas Eve. Four hundred strangers flocked to his little casket and surrounded his tiny body with stuffed animals. When I wasn't writing about Isaiah, I was watching Ronnie descend into a deep darkness.

FOR CHRISTMAS I got him a hunting book and a video-store gift certificate. Through me, Mom sent thirty dollars in cash. He gave me two twenty-dollar bills in an envelope on which he touchingly wrote "Pie." He had little to say. I'd take him on drives, but he remained hopeless. He didn't say it, but his disappointment with Max must have felt like the many times Mom let him down. He was burping and swigging antacid.

By New Year's, I wondered if he was passing blood or if his eyesight might be fading because he was paler, more lumbering. He said only that he was tired. In the final stages of acromegaly, muscle weakness and congestive heart failure are common. Hunched over, with his head hung low as he perched on his stool, his arms draped over the empty barber chair, he resembled a vulture. When I heard Ronnie, ever the diplomat as a barber, snarling at longtime customers, I knew for sure that he'd given up.

He refused to see Will Truslow for checkups. Behind the scenes, Will was rushing to arrange free surgery for Ronnie. An endocrinologist at the National Institutes of Health in Bethesda, Maryland, was offering a free operation. NIH would pay for Ronnie's travel. I laid it out, but Ronnie said no

way. I offered to drive him to Bethesda for a consult. "Don't you think you ought to at least see about this?"

"Yeah," he replied, as he sat forlornly in his shop, staring out the window at the street scene. "And I ought to be president of that bank over there, and I ought to have a home and a loving wife, and I ought to have gotten my inheritance from Max."

IN MID-JANUARY, MY cat Rural Earl was hit by a car in front of my house. For days I rushed home each lunch break to syringe liquid food through a stomach tube in his neck. Earl, in pain from a broken jaw, growled at me as I helped him. I was getting nothing but flak from the two crotchety males in my life.

The NIH doctor called me with details. Ronnie would receive $100,000 worth of free treatment—exactly the amount, oddly, he'd counted on from Max. Then he'd follow a strict regimen: Every day for six weeks he'd drive himself to radiation at a Roanoke medical office. And for five years, he'd inject himself with hormones three or four times a day. I didn't tell Ronnie any of the postoperative stuff. It was a deal breaker. I couldn't imagine him trusting doctors enough, or caring about himself enough, to do any of that.

First I had to get him to go meet the surgeon. If by any chance Ronnie hit it off with the man, the rest might follow. The doctor was busy. He was impatient when I explained Ronnie's distrust of authority figures like him. But this surgery was our only hope. Ronnie wasn't budging. "Aw, we'll get there one of these days," he told me wearily. He couldn't serve two masters at once—the doctors he owed money to and the ones who wanted to operate on him again.

On February 9, I took the NIH consent form by the bar-

bershop in hopes Ronnie would sign it. He wouldn't even look at it. He threw it in the trash. I retrieved it.

His belly was in an uproar. He was nauseated. Bottles of Pepto-Bismol and Mylanta sat all around the barbershop. He was rising in the middle of the night to gobble bowls of cereal to calm his storming gut. He had so little energy that it took fifteen to twenty minutes to work up the steam at day's end to close the barbershop and walk a few short yards around the corner to his Ramcharger. I left for Charlottesville. I had to start my fellowship. I'd be back often, I promised Ronnie.

I SPENT THE next few days in a courthouse, gathering names of people sent decades earlier to one of Virginia's mental hospitals with plans to sterilize them. The next weekend, I went home, sorted mail, took care of my cats, and saw friends. Monday afternoon, February 18, I went by the barbershop on my way back to Charlottesville. The lights were out. The door was locked. Through the window I saw the gray hair of Ronnie's aging clientele covering the floor. Ronnie must have felt too rotten to sweep it up. I had to leave. I didn't go by his house.

Late the next morning, that Tuesday, Thelma came by Ronnie's house to check on something. His cars were out back. She hollered up the stairs. When she got no answer, she went next door. Alpha came over and peeked in Ronnie's door and knew right away he was dead. Ronnie had been fully dressed and ready to go to work that Monday when I'd gone to the shop looking for him.

Medics estimated he'd been dead at least twelve to eighteen hours. He'd lain close to death most of Monday. Alpha called the newspaper. My editor reached me at the humanities

center. I rushed across town in Charlottesville to tell Mom, who looked stricken, then sped the two hours to Vinton. The one time I should have gone by his house, I hadn't.

HE'D BLED TO death from the rectum. The official cause of death was an arrhythmia brought on by gastrointestinal bleeding. He was sitting up in bed with a bulb still burning in a reading lamp clamped to the vertical supports of his headboard. Medics found thick rubber-banded rolls of cash, $6,400 all told, scattered around his body and peeking from within blankets. His mattress was soaked with blood.

If I'd gone to the house the day before, I might have gotten him to the emergency room in time. I'll never know. He might have begged off medical attention the way he had with Max in April, but I would have called 911 anyway. Still he was much weaker. Another abdominal surgery might have killed him. But I should have been there. I should have tried.

TO RONNIE, PREACHERS were nothing but deceivers and scoundrels. When my friend Bob, a United Methodist minister, came to Max's funeral, Ronnie scolded me later: "Why'd you send that preacher around here?" Ronnie didn't know that for years Bob and his wife had listened to me agonize over Ronnie. A progressive sort of minister, Bob wanted only to comfort Ronnie, not slap his name on some list of saved souls. After Max's service, Ronnie noticed Bob about to drive off and told Bob he admired his "unit," his car. Bob had chuckled ever since about Ronnie's fifties talk. He offered to do Ronnie's service.

That mild, sunny Thursday morning, a dozen or more of Ronnie's customers came with their wives to stand by his grave, a few paces from the cemetery road where Ronnie used to walk in the evenings. At least one of the women he'd cursed at his favorite restaurant was there. She and her coworkers sent flowers and a card signed "The Girls." Four of Mom's cousins came, three members of the Hicks family who'd been her friends all her life, and ten of my newspaper colleagues. As we settled into the service, my eyes took in the far-off peaks of the Allegheny and the Blue Ridge Mountains.

In his eulogy, Bob pointed to the gravestones around us. Ronnie knew hundreds of those people. "He listened to their stories, their problems, their jokes, their woes. And likewise he touched their lives with his replies—replies filled with depth, character, meaning, and experience." Ronnie might have thought of himself as a loner, but for three decades he served the people of his town as faithfully as anyone.

I thought that day that if I hadn't procured a copy of my birth certificate, if I hadn't read every word of it, and if Mom hadn't come clean with me about whom the numeral "1" on that form referred to, I might never have known Ronnie was my brother. If I hadn't sought him out in 1987 and gotten to know him, if I hadn't been with him in the hospital—if none of those ifs had happened and Mom had told me my "cousin" Ronnie had died—I might not have even gone to the funeral of this relative I barely knew. Then the lies would have been compounded, and Mom would have lived out the rest of her life knowing that not only had she failed to ease Ronnie's anguish over his childhood, but she'd also cheated me out of the truth. She would have withheld an essential part of herself from the people she held most dear.

PART VI

LEARNING STILL

Unearthing Ronnie

Ronnie's Sportsman Barber Shop was a fixture of
downtown Vinton, Virginia, for thirty years.
Photo courtesy of Don Petersen

I thought I'd be able to pack Ronnie away now, mentally
and otherwise. But his landlord at the barbershop was
pushing me to clean it out so he could rent it to a new bar-
ber. Research on other people would have to wait. Ronnie's
belongings, bearing clues to his story, were irresistible. I
used the landlord's pressure as an excuse to dig in.

I started sifting through it the day after the funeral. Prac-
tically everything Ronnie touched wound up on the floors
of his bedroom, his kitchen, his cars, his barbershop, and its
back room. Signs of what he cared most about rested among
the fast-food wrappers and the antihistamine bottles. Wooden

turkey calls with chalk to create friction on the lids and fine sandpaper to abrade them when the lids no longer took chalk. Flashlights by the score. Car registrations from the sixties. Hundreds of black-and-white photographs of snakes, bears, and paw prints. The dust of thirty years rose up and coated my throat.

As miserable as he was toward the end, Ronnie was still reading about history and about turkey hunting. I knew that for sure because he used recent medical bills as bookmarks. I found a young woman's diary with the locking clasp broken off. I found tiny, torn bits of paper throughout the piles bearing Max's name and phone number written in Ronnie's hand, always askew and always without capitals or hyphens: "home max 242 1754." Wherever he went, if something went wrong, whoever found him would know where he belonged.

I counted two hundred pairs of chukkas, Hush Puppies, and other shoes in several sizes for his growing feet. Almost as many pairs of slacks, many brand-new. Countless jockey shorts and brown socks, also new. In his sickest years Ronnie kept buying more rather than do laundry. A green duffel bag, three feet long and stuffed with clean but age-yellowed jockeys, sat at the bottom of a wardrobe. Weary, I almost pitched the whole bag, but from within the fiber popped two handguns and, rolled up in plaid boxers, a plastic rye bread bag containing three rubber-banded money rolls, $1,000 each. Here and there in the bedroom—between the medics first, then me—we found $12,000.

His illness left behind six or more blood pressure cuffs, books on diabetes and hypertension, and, stuffed in the pockets of every garment, tissues, napkins, and paper towels. I

discovered a Ronnie-style order to his bedroom—down vests here, khakis there. Behind a dusty armchair heaped high with stuff was a tall cluster of brown paper bags, each marked by year, and within, white envelopes containing notes of a day's earnings: "August 1985, $56, $30, $38, $42, $39, $69, $22 . . ." I could see him heading to his taxman every spring with the previous year's brown bag under his arm. Ronnie was trying to be a good boy.

But the barbershop was vile from his sickened neglect. The sterilizer in which he plunged his shears and combs in alcohol was rusting and hadn't been changed in a very long time. The first aid cabinet coughed up a three-pack of Trojan rubbers, one missing. Along shelves furry with hair clippings was a stack of *Playboys* from the eighties.

I brought home a videocassette and played it, hoping it might be a home movie. It was a bootleg porn flick.

I found a Rolex engraved in 1984 as a birthday gift to an unknown man. A jeweler confirmed it was counterfeit. Deep in the piles, I unearthed JOB rolling papers, matches, and a stainless steel hemostat, the surgical forceps people use as a roach clip. I didn't find any pot, but Ronnie must have tried it. He left behind no tobacco or alcohol. I never saw him drink beer, wine, or anything alcoholic.

In his bedroom, I discovered guns, lots and lots of guns. Receipts showed that Ronnie had been buying and trading firearms for decades. But the day I had come to his bedroom to pick up Ronnie's funeral outfit, as I searched for clean socks, I'd noticed a fancy bone-handled handgun in the masses of clothes. I never saw that gun again. Someone knew it was there and by the time I arrived to process his stuff, they'd

come for it and only it. Max's family reported no break-ins. I never learned who took it, but knowing someone had been there spooked me as I labored.

Ronnie's kitchen was a mycology lab. Fresh-ground Kroger peanut butter from long ago had molded, dried, and cracked within its plastic tubs like desiccated lake beds. Cans of beans had sat in his corner cabinet for so many years that they exploded, rotted, molded, and turned to dust. Didn't he and Max hear those cans popping and wonder what the heck it was?

The year before, when I came for his identification cards, I'd noticed two brown stains between vertical supports of the headboard of his iron bed. I figured an overheated bulb in his clip-on reading lamp had scorched the wall. But on closer inspection, I now saw that scalp oil, probably mixed with hair tonic, had built up over many years at two side-by-side spots where he rested his head. A piece of the rust-colored accumulation had become so thick it fell away, exposing a bit of the wall's underlying plaster. These very rooms had given up hope.

RONNIE LEFT NO will. Over the next year and a half, I gathered his savings and cash, sold his cars, his remaining fourteen guns, and his barber chairs, and paid off $52,000 of his $84,000 in medical bills. I wrenched my back carrying a sixty-five-pound metal bucket of change out of his bedroom. Filtering out the tiny brown buttons from his khaki pants pockets and the ever-present bits of hair, I wrapped thousands of coins in paper sleeves at home in the evenings and deposited every single penny into Ronnie's estate account.

Dumb ass, I could hear him say, *grab some of that for yourself. Don't give it all to The·Man.* I took what I cared about—a Flattopper comb, two old razor strops, his books, his turkey calls, and his bags of pictures and papers, with battalions of tiny light-brown roaches streaming beneath it all.

As I drove back and forth between Vinton and Roanoke, I began to see Ronnie-like figures everywhere—tall, dejected-looking men, often sitting stoically behind the steering wheel of an old car or walking down the street, their long soles slapping the sidewalk. The reporter in me was running down, and the sister was kicking in. Our common smell was stronger than ever—so many of his things were at my house now—but I didn't mind anymore. His scent meant he was still with me and he still had things to show me.

THE SALVATION ARMY hauled away a pickup load of Ronnie's best suede coats, barely worn tweed jackets, and other high-quality clothes. For Ronnie and for our mama, clothes were prosperity markers, attainable when fancy cars and houses were beyond their reach. Mom equated a sharp dresser with respectability, cleanliness, and morality. Ronnie may have picked that up from her. Within his mounds, I found a navy-blue V-neck wool sweater she'd mailed him one Christmas, still store-folded in white tissue paper and in its shallow gift box.

Some of his cash probably went away in the pocket of one of those donated jackets. I couldn't search through every one of thousands of garments. It seemed right, anyway, that some man looking for a warm coat might reach into a pocket and come out with a hundred-dollar bill, like Ronnie winning it

big with that racehorse. The most heartbreaking sight as I dumped debris at a landfill from a friend's truck was Ronnie's bloody mattress lying lonely on the ground.

That spring, my folks came to visit. Daddy had watched as I labored on Ronnie's behalf. He'd cashed one of his $450 paychecks from two weeks of work at the farm supply. "Here, Pie. Take this." He bit his quivering lip. The money came in handy as the estate lawyer filed for refunds for landfill fees and other expenses.

Without examining much of Ronnie's materials, I packed away what I hadn't sold and schlepped boxes to the attic. Someday I'd study it all. Right then, I had research deadlines to make and aging parents to watch over.

Our Family Shrivels

My favorite picture of my parents, which I took
on their sixtieth anniversary at their home in
Charlottesville, Virginia.

I long felt bad I hadn't given my parents grandchildren.
But a few years after Ronnie died, I did the next best
thing: I married Dan Crawford, a man they loved like a son.

Simple happiness was not ours for long. In 2003, after
a difficult, protracted battle with emphysema, my father
passed away. Mom's anxieties skittered higher after that,
and her faith in the world plunged beneath her aching knees.
She was frightened of spoiled food, any criticisms, poverty,
car accidents, falling, my death, curvy roads, strong winds,
snakes, making mistakes, looking shabby, snow, ice, strang-
ers, fire, losing control of herself, embarrassment, cheese
(causes constipation), green vegetables (interfere with blood

thinner), salt (raises blood pressure), and surprises (even pleasant ones).

One of my rewards for washing her back and scrubbing her toilet was clarification of family history. When I was little, she'd storm red-faced around the house, angry about Daddy's friendships with the Keswick postmistress and with the church pianist. Now I could ask, Had he fooled around with those women? "No, he was just being friendly. He was nice to everybody. I thought they misunderstood. He could be a flirt."

Even in our saddest months, Mom made me laugh. At the annual service that honored deceased patients of Daddy's hospice, an aged clarinetist played a series of doleful classical pieces in a random, modern pattern. When he was done, Mom blurted out for all to hear, "I'm glad they cut that noise off." Don't know what she thought it was, but it wasn't music.

In a talk about heaven, Mom declared the idea of life after death to be "bullshit." As a young girl, she'd taken the invitational walk of salvation down the aisle at Bethlehem Church. A woman pressured her to, promising she'd see her mother again. Even then, Mom said, still bitter, "I knew that was baloney."

WITH MY HAND at her waist as she rose the two painful steps to her back door, I felt the grinding of Mom's knee bones telegraphing up her frame. Getting in and out of her Buick Century was agony and sometimes impossible. New drugs interfered with her blood thinner, and she injured a leg vein. Blood pooled inside and all around her ankle. She could barely stand. My longtime doctor had gently ushered Daddy through death and would do the same for Mom. As he knelt by her red, swollen ankle in his examining room, Mom as-

sured him, "You can take my shoe off. I washed my feet." She
still believed she stunk.

HER FORMERLY COIFFED hair now Einstein wild, Mom was
as adamantly anti-science as Ronnie. We couldn't convince
her that her thermal pane windows would keep out the cold.
On a Christmas card–like day, with blue-white snow drap-
ing the trees, kids on sleds, and cardinals darting to feeders
Dan had erected for her, we opened her curtains to reveal the
cheery scene. She insisted on closing them.

Two nights after a hospital stay when doctors studied her
pains and loss of appetite, Dan and I went to dinner across
town. When we checked on Mom at nine o'clock, her bed-
room door was closed. She always kept it open for her cat.
"Mary Carter," she said faintly as I approached, "I'm on the
floor. I can't get up." She'd fallen while setting her glasses on
the dresser and landed against the inside of the door. A thin
female medic squeezed in. Through the crack, I spied Mom's
splayed left foot. She'd broken her left hip. She'd fractured her
right one six years earlier.

OVER THE NEXT thirteen months, Mom and I rode the
troughs and swells of old age. She brought to it all her many
fears, a deep loathing of her body, her residual shame from
her youthful pregnancy, and a cognitive disconnect that made
her a dangerous patient. While in the hospital recovering from
hip surgery, she insisted she could stand and walk without
assistance. I had to keep an eye on her or she'd take off down
the hall and dislodge the new metal ball in her hip socket. I

begged her to relax, to which she aptly replied, "I'm not made that way."

She went into a nursing home, where imagery of her country upbringing emerged poetically as she recovered from the anesthesia. She hallucinated scenes of lambs playing in fields. The bellowing of a female patient was a calf hollering for its mama. The trilling of the phone at the nurses' station was the whirring of a screech owl. When she had diarrhea, she asked for a slop jar, which is what old-timers called a bedpan.

DAY AFTER DAY, as she steadily declined, she lay in bed grieving for herself.

"I feel so, so . . ."

"So *what*, Mom?"

"I feel so guilty."

"For what?"

"I don't know."

WE MOVED HER to a private corner room with two windows. One of her earlier roommates, a wise little woman with a lyrical tongue, had told us she knew just what to do for an old person: "They need a pillow for every bone." I brought in colorful cushions and decorated the room with Mom's cherished pictures, plants, and tchotchkes. A few years before he died, following a squabble with Daddy, she'd burned his love letters from their courting days. But now, to each of the four framed photos of him, she'd proclaim daily, "I love you." When I set out her photo portrait taken shortly before their wedding, she stared at it awhile and remarked, "I think I look sad."

AT THE END of her life, Mom still bemoaned the fact that she had sinned in having Ronnie. When she announced to me these three words, just three syllables—"I'm no good"—she seemed to be expressing the judgment of herself she'd borne throughout her adult life.

Though she'd earlier rejected the idea of heaven, now, like the proverbial believer in the foxhole, she was hoping for it. "Do you think I'll be with Daddy?" That's how she referred to him when speaking to me. She was sure he'd been whisked straight through the pearly gates, no need for examination. Though I wasn't much of a believer, I assured her that yes, she would be with Daddy. I told her she'd been a good woman.

"No, I haven't."

ON A FRIDAY morning, she was going. Phlegm crackled in her chest. Soft wheezes with her every breath were seabird cries in the distance. I knelt by her bed and kissed her, held her hand, stroked her arms. As she was slipping away that afternoon, Dan and her church friends came to kiss her goodbye.

Her minister, who'd watched so many people die, advised me to take note as her breathing slowed. This was once-in-a-lifetime business. All the troubles of her life will melt away, he told me, all her conflicts and worries. It will all boil down to her being barely there and then not there at all.

As she fed Mom morphine, a nurse skated the chestpiece of her stethoscope over Mom's heart. An aide kept an eye on the faint pulsing of a blood vessel on the left side of her neck. The three of us hovered head-to-head as Mom's tongue lolled

around near her bottom teeth. In her right ear I whispered, "I love you, Mom." Then she was gone.

Aides came to wash her body and wrap it in a white sheet. The staff closed patients' doors along the hallway as two black-suited undertakers wheeled her away on a maroon-draped gurney.

Thirty minutes after she died, I gathered up her pillows. The one that had been under her left hip to relieve pressure on a bedsore was still warm. I shuddered slightly at this ghostly, unexpected touch, then wished I could keep it forever. The lingering heat of my mother's body was another farewell, though not her last.

A FINER SIFTING

I Draw Closer

Mom took this photo as Ronnie approached his
first birthday. It likely was taken at the Crittenton
Home for unwed mothers in Lynchburg, Virginia.

Those first years without Ronnie, Mom, and Daddy, I set
about healing myself. I took a road trip to Minnesota.
I moved to a new house. I formed a writers' group called
FUMA (Fire Under My Ass) to make myself start writing.
I was desperate to understand my mother and Ronnie the
only way I knew how, through reporting, through writing,
through working out on the page the greatest mystery of
my life.

On visits with Hicks family elders, I learned the names
of Grandpa Emmett's workhorses, the circumstances of him
sawing off his fingers, the jokes about his prayers flapping

about in the church ceiling, and the layout of the cabin where Miss Belle had her privates peppered. Other people told me about Ronnie's Romeo ways in his twenties, his accident with a motorcycle, his grumpiness with waitresses, his hobnobbing with rich golfers.

I went back to the boxes and scrutinized everything he and Mom left behind, each time with a finer sieve, each time revealing yet another layer. I found Mom's faded keepsake book where girlhood friends wrote sentimental rhymes about kisses, death, and husbands to come. Two years before she was pregnant with Ronnie, she penned there a list of her nine favorite songs. At the top was "Picture on the Wall," recorded by country music pioneers the Carter Family, from farther down in the mountains of Southwest Virginia.

> There's an old and faded picture on the wall
> That has been a-hanging there for many years
> It's a picture of my mother
> For I know there is no other
> That can take the place of mother on the wall

Listening online to the Depression-era recording, I could imagine Mom's soprano catching on a line near the end: *Since I lost that dear old mother years ago / There is none to which with troubles I can go.*

Months before she died, Mom told me this: "If my mama had lived, I wouldn't have gotten into trouble. Wouldn't have gotten into trouble." She said it a third time, as if in a mourning chant. *Wouldn't have gotten into trouble.*

I TRACKED DOWN old friends from Keswick, people of my parents' generation. One of the women had arrived in the community shortly after they'd carted Ronnie off to Western State. She was shocked to learn about Mom's hidden-away boy. "I just can't believe that about your mother." She sat back in her chair and stared at me awhile before saying it again, with emphasis this time on the "*your* mother," as if to say "*your* mother, of all the women in the world." I knew what she meant. Mom presented herself as starchy and beyond reproach. Her prudish exterior was a cover-up. "Yep," Dan said when I told him what the woman said. "Your mom was a recovering fallen woman."

I found men who'd grown up in Keswick with Ronnie. One who lived at the manor house where Ronnie often stole food from the kitchen remembered his parents ordering him and his brothers to stay away from Ronnie. But they couldn't resist him and his freedoms. He was easygoing and fun to be around. Plus, he was so obviously lonely. "This was a person," his old pal recalled, "who wanted attention so much it was crazy."

ONLY RECENTLY I took a careful look at the stack of get-well cards Ronnie received when he was in the hospital in 1990. A customer joked that Ronnie had better recover soon or all his clients would resemble sheepdogs. Another must not have known Ronnie's last name because he addressed his card simply to "Mr. Slim." "I seen your card in the Barber Shop Window that said you liked to get cards. Im one of your customers but you probably don't know me. I always say clippers on the sides is OK with me Maybe that will ring a bell.

I don't know what happened but I hope you get well soon. I am sending a little money and I hope it wont make you mad or hurt your pride. I know it gets pretty rough when you are sick I just got out of the hospital in October 1988 I had a lung cancer operation and I still don't breathe very good. Well hang in there and get well."

OF ALL THE things Ronnie left behind, none was so revealing as the 1959–1960 diary of a teenaged girl. Its plastic back was decorated in a diamond argyle pattern in black and cream, with tiny fleur-de-lis symbols inside each diamond. The back metal clasp of its locking device had been ripped off. Why would Ronnie have this, and why would he keep it?

As I examined the little book, I saw that it was the diary kept by his first love. Ronnie didn't often admit to soft feelings for anyone, but this girl had stayed in his mind until he died. "I would have given both my legs and my soul for her," Ronnie told me, with more conviction than I'd ever heard him speak of anything. She was seventeen and eighteen when she kept the journal.

Maybe I could find her. Maybe I could learn how Ronnie handled close relationships. Watching him during barbershop visits and hearing his many suspicions about people, I had trouble picturing him being truly close to anyone. Was the remoteness I saw in him related to his physical problems of more recent years? Or were its roots deeper, earlier?

In the spring of 2010, I found two listings in the local phone book for people with the diary keeper's unusual last name. One of them was her brother. He gave me her married name and her phone number. She was as eager as I to talk about

Ronnie. Over many fruit plates at her favorite restaurant over the next few years, she shared such intimate details of their relationship that I won't name her here. She looked like a Joyce to me, so that's what I'll call her.

Joyce was seventeen and soon to graduate from high school the day she met Ronnie, March 26, 1959. She met him at Polly's house after the funeral service for Roy. She thought Ronnie was charming, courteous, well dressed. He was twenty-three.

A brown-haired girl still round with baby fat, Joyce had kissed boys she'd met through her ultraconservative church, but she was still a virgin. Ronnie was gentlemanly and tender with her. He took her shopping for a bracelet in downtown Roanoke, and when she couldn't choose between the gold one and the silver, he bought her both. He loaned her a record player and bought her records by the 101 Strings, an orchestra that pumped out the romantic mood music they listened to when they made out.

But as their courtship progressed, Joyce told me, Ronnie began to pressure her sexually, sometimes seeming as though he was on the edge of violence. Eventually, she relented, but she always felt that the more ambivalent she was, the more he pressured her, as though he feared she might leave him and he had to seize what he could. Even though she felt somewhat coerced, there was still sweetness in their relationship.

In the fall of 1959, Joyce left home for her freshman year at a small Midwestern college run by her Pentecostal denomination. In January, when he drove her to the train for her return to school after the Christmas holidays, they had sex in his car at the railroad station. Once again, it was get it while you can. Despite Ronnie's aggression, Joyce continued to see him.

He sent her two dollars a month at school for movies and

school incidentals. He visited her mother on weekends while Joyce was gone. Ronnie liked to enter Joyce's house through the back door, near her bedroom, and hang out back there. Joyce's mother often shooed him away. She found him intrusive, pushy, disrespectful of boundaries. Joyce's mother warned her that he was overbearing. He had come to their fundamentalist church a few times and rudely interrupted Bible lessons to argue with members' views on the gospel. That embarrassed Joyce.

He never mentioned his biological mother. Joyce didn't even know he had a half sister. Ronnie did offer one clue to his origins. While she was at college and going to many movies, he suggested she see the just-released *Home from the Hill*. "Ronnie said it was practically the story of his life. . . . He said, 'You'll understand a lot if you'll just go see that movie.'" So she did, and later, I ordered it from Netflix.

The lead character, played by George Peppard, is the illegitimate son of a wealthy Texas cotton planter. The story revolves around contention between that son and the landowner's spoiled legitimate one. In a dramatic encounter between the two, the bastard son contrasts his measly life with the opulence surrounding the other man's:

> *You know, I was hanging around the day they named*
> *you in church, hanging around the ice cream and*
> *birthday cake parties they gave you every year of your*
> *life, hanging around on the Fourth of July when they set*
> *off firecrackers for you, when they gave you ponies and*
> *an electric train, when they drove you up and down the*
> *main street of town in an open touring car so everybody*
> *could see the son and heir. Somewhere along the*
> *way . . . I got a notion I had some of that coming to me.*

Ronnie heard echoes of his own life. I was the one who was dressed up and shown off to the neighbors. Buddy was given any toy he desired. At first, when Ronnie was with Polly and Roy, he had a pony and an electric train too, but eventually he was left in the shadows, just like the man in the movie.

RONNIE'S ROUGH WAYS continued to baffle Joyce. "I love him," she wrote in her diary in March 1960, "but he makes it so hard for me." Ronnie was talking seriously about marrying her. Her diary indicates she was considering it, though she was getting other proposals too. That April, slightly more than a year after she met Ronnie, a young man Joyce's mother preferred over Ronnie took Joyce out for a Coke. Joyce said it wasn't a real date, but Ronnie's Chevy was parked in the driveway when the man drove Joyce home.

When he saw Joyce with the stranger, Ronnie flew into a rage. Red-faced, he stormed into her bedroom. He grabbed her record player and records and threw them into the trunk of his car. He must have taken her diary that day too because her entries suddenly ceased that month. Ronnie stormed off. Joyce never saw him again. She told me that if Ronnie had returned and talked it over with her—and if he'd sincerely declared his love—she might very well have married him. Joyce's father reported the theft of the diary to the police, but because it was of no monetary value, they convinced him to drop the charge.

According to the diary, Ronnie told Joyce he wanted no children until they'd been married for at least five years. At one point, Joyce's period was three months late. She spent days at college terrified she was pregnant. He wrote her not

to worry about it, perhaps because he hoped to marry her anyway.

Years later, however, Ronnie told me he had never wanted children. He tucked condoms in his car and even in the holes of trees in the woods where he had sex with his girlfriends. His explanation made my heart hurt: "I didn't want to create any more bastards like me." I believe he realized that he wasn't emotionally able to commit to marriage, and he didn't want to saddle anyone with fatherless children like him.

What interested me most about Joyce's diary was that when Ronnie seized it, he read what he could of it and jotted comments on many pages in which Joyce mentioned him. I recognized his handwriting. His commentary was the dialogue he was never able to have face-to-face with Joyce. He yearns for a deep connection, it is clear, but he doesn't know how to achieve it or how to keep it.

> When Joyce notes that she's just written Ronnie a letter "telling him I wanted more respect," Ronnie writes, "Love is respect."
> When she laments that she "wished I had someone to love me truly," Ronnie writes, "I do."
> When she says she wrote to Ronnie to ask him not to come to see her anymore but then lacked the nerve to mail it, Ronnie writes, "she is using me."
> When she says she asked a pastor for advice on how to get rid of Ronnie, Ronnie writes, "ask me not him."
> When Joyce has a change of heart and decides she does want to see Ronnie, he writes, "that [sic] more like it."
> When she's having trouble with her studies and wishes

Ronnie were there to "love me some," Ronnie writes,
 "I love you honey."
When she writes that she doesn't think Ronnie is
 interested in marriage any longer, Ronnie writes, "you
 are wrong about that."
And when she's flunking a course and says, "I wish I were
 dead. Why I was ever born I'll never know," Ronnie
 writes, "to be my wife."

Instead, Joyce married the man who took her out for that
Coke. Ronnie told me that years after he sped away from
Joyce's house, he saw her in a store with young children and
obviously pregnant with another. She has no memory of that
encounter, but by then, Ronnie's appearance had changed so
much because of the acromegaly that she wouldn't have rec-
ognized him.

THERE WAS ONLY one other person in the world who knew
my parents and Ronnie. This man met my mom seven years
before I did. Before I was born, he was present at our tenant
house the day that apprehensive eight-year-old Ronnie ar-
rived from the orphanage.

John Sharpless "Buddy" McIntyre Jr. was as moored in
my family as in his own. He practically fell out of his moth-
er's womb and into my mother's arms. If Mom couldn't find
a babysitter, little Buddy accompanied Mom and Daddy on
their earliest dates. I went to Mississippi twice to see Buddy,
a retired insurance broker. I'd known him all my life because
he maintained such a close relationship with Mom and Daddy,

writing them hundreds of letters, sending them checks that made them financially secure, and visiting them whenever he returned home to Virginia. But Buddy and I had never spoken about Ronnie. I wasn't even sure if he knew Ronnie was Mom's son.

On my first visit, I saw in Buddy the subtle gestures and body language of my parents—the way he tilted his head, the way he laughed. I heard them in his voice, in his figures of speech, and in his tender heart. When I mentioned it to Buddy's wife, Carolyn, on our walk back from their gardens, she said, "Well, of course. He spent more time with your folks than anybody."

He chokes with fondness when he speaks of Daddy and of "AID-drah," as he pronounces Mom's name. He saw the best of my folks. He was a grown man before his mother told him that Ronnie was Mom's son, and he said he admired my father for "overlooking all that."

Still, even as a little boy, Buddy wondered why Early was so hard on Ronnie. "He cut him no slack. He was always on him. I never understood it, because Early was such a good man. It made no sense to me." My parents raised a fine man. It just wasn't Ronnie.

YEARS AFTER MOM died, I read her very last letters to Ronnie, which he'd hidden away. Six times over his last nine months, she begged him to have the surgery and to save himself. "Please let them try and help you. I'm sure they can." By November, three months before his death, she was pleading. "*Please*," she wrote, underlining the word, "see somebody who can take care of that tumor." In a note card adorned with

drawings of seashells and postmarked twenty-two days be-
fore he died, she offered to help him pay for the operation.

That Christmas, she sent a card and a church directory pic-
ture of her and Daddy. She invited Ronnie to their house for
Christmas Day. Now I know that back when she'd seemed so
emotionally frozen, she was always quietly hurting for him.
On a small sheet of writing paper inside the card, she wrote,
"We are getting older and don't have a lot of time left, so why
not make peace and enjoy each other?" As far as I know, he
never replied.

Walking with Them

Ronnie must have been around twelve in this
snapshot our mother took in the side yard of our
tenant house on Bridlespur Farm.

There were many things Ronnie never knew about Mom, things I learned about only after he died: The diaper-pinning incident that flung him into the foster care system, for instance. Polly and Roy's crusade to adopt him. The years of squabbling between Mom and Polly over his care. The constant guilt-inflicting push from the orphanage head for Mom to reclaim Ronnie, which probably snuffed out Polly's chances of adoption. The pressure on Mom from wealthy Keswick landowners to rein Ronnie in, and Mom's fears that we'd all be thrown off the farm. I know now that she sent him to the asylum to protect me and to preserve our home.

As her sheltered child, I can say her choice remains a horror to me and must have been for her.

I think often of an incident at my folks' house in Charlottesville. Outside their kitchen door was a roofed patio where Mom and Daddy stored mops, brooms, and gardening tools. Mom kept terra-cotta flowerpots there in a rusted tool cabinet. She opened its creaky door one spring to discover a mouse cringing beside her worm-sized offspring. "Mary Carter, that mouse's eyes said, 'Please don't hurt my baby.'" Mom closed the cabinet, found something else to plant her begonias in, and restored their peace. That mouse's eyes stayed with my hyper-maternal mom for years, and she told the story many times. What I might have read as sheer fear, Mom saw as one mother's appeal to another. The role of mother was holy to Mom. After the death of her mother, the women of the Hicks family brought her up almost as an add-on to their own large broods. Those strong, warmhearted women remained her models for mothering all her life. The fact that Ronnie got so little of her must have ground into Mom. In the Adria Bishop Code of Conduct, she had committed the ultimate sin: She had failed to love her own child.

AMONG THE PHOTOS of Ronnie I find most ironic is one that Mom took in our side yard when he was about twelve. The leaves are off the trees, and Ronnie's wearing his signature ball cap, plaid wool jacket, and surprisingly, jodhpurs, the riding pants that in the 1940s version flared dramatically at the hips. Ronnie dressed in hunting clothes mostly. But he must have found these horsey pants, probably ripped or

stained, in a horse barn's trash, or maybe one of his better-off
buddies gave him their hand-me-downs. He looks comical in
his mountain boy duds with those fancy pants.

The picture led me to think about the role Ronnie played
in my folks' acute sense of abasement in Keswick. They were
self-conscious there anyway, surrounded as they were by
such affluent neighbors. The unspoken rule was that servant
families were to be exceptionally cautious and servile. To act
otherwise was to break a tradition stretching back centuries.
Ronnie flaunted all the wrong qualities for Keswick. His ir-
reverent spying and thieving pricked my folks' separate roots
of self-contempt. He was a rebel amid a compliant workforce,
as well as a daily reminder of Mom's girlish transgression.
It must have been odd to see him walking along the narrow
highway, a skinny, raggedy kid with his thumb out, heading
into town for a caddying shift. All Daddy's fellow farmhands
and everybody we knew from church, store, and school trav-
eled that highway. I can hear what they must have said as they
steered past Ronnie and twisted their necks for a closer look:
*Isn't that boy some kin to Adria Bishop? Why's she let him
roam around like that?*

As he wandered Keswick's estates doing his mischief, Ron-
nie was that fly dancing around on the ox horn. He was a
child trying to provoke the unfeeling cartilage of his blood
kin. He was trying to win his mother's admiration, but in all
the wrong ways. *Mama, look at me! Don't you see how clever
and resourceful I am? How strong I am? Mama, please reach
out to me! Okay, well, the heck with you; I'll show you. I'll
make my own money. I'll build my own house. I'll buy my
own food. I'll show you that I'll be fine without you. I don't
need you at all.*

LOVE ALWAYS HAS its enemies, even in the best of circumstances. Predators are poised to pounce in an instant of inattention. With Ronnie, both the boy and the man, each time the prospect of tender attachment came back around toward him, some weak-kneed person, some coldhearted somebody, some kind of fear, some kind of shame, some sort of rigid religiosity, some economic or emotional poverty, or Ronnie's own self-defeating distrust would rise up and drive it away. All those foes of good-heartedness succeeded in killing Ronnie. Foremost among them was our family affliction, a thorough habit of shame and self-hatred.

His story was one of love interrupted. His closest people turned that tap of benevolence on and off so many times, Ronnie became disillusioned and decided to stick to himself. In his aloneness, with no one paying attention, he was pulled down by an illness that ended his life prematurely. In the end, I would disappoint him too, like everybody else.

Our bond was new and tentative. I became a voyeur of this fascinating brother-self. He was me if I'd been deprived of the love that shaped me. But studying someone is not closeness. Studying a subject means that you hold them apart, and except for the months when Ronnie was most unwell, when I felt genuine hope for his future, I maintained a certain distance from him. I didn't reveal much of myself to him. We'd traveled in such different circles that I didn't think he'd relate to my thinking, my joys, my politics. He never asked much about me because more than anything, he needed to be heard.

At first I was fixated on the crust that acromegaly had hardened on him, as well as the crust of his profanity, racism,

anger, and disappointment. I wanted to see the undefended Ronnie, the one behind his crusts, and I wanted to see Mom behind hers too. But neither of them opened up to me entirely about what thoughts punished them in the dark nights as they lay sleepless in their beds. What they were dealing with remained unresolved within them and between them.

Ronnie preferred to stay sarcastic and jocular with me, a guy who was way too cool for any school. He was a lofty tree, lower limbs hacked off, trunk toughened by his seasons, upper branches wide and bushy, laughing in the sun, smirking down on the rest of us, and secretly wishing he could be a part of the contented lives he imagined most other people had. As he said, he should have been president of that bank. He should have had that home and that loving wife.

AS I WRITE these final painful paragraphs, I see Mom's and Ronnie's very similar faces blown up large in my memory. Their eyes, noses, and facial bones were so much alike, even after his features had been exaggerated by disease. I see the way each of them looked at me in their woundedness, in their grumpiness. The way each of them, in the end, laid many of their secrets before me. The way Mom seemed to hate for me to learn what brought her down. The way Ronnie hoped I might bring him some final sisterly comradeship, unimagined by him for so long. The way it hurt for them to watch me wrestling with the histories they'd hidden away. I was their precious Mary Carter, the girl they called Pie, the one they long had shielded from their misfortunes, the one ultimately spared their drama. What could sheltered little Pie do for them at this late stage?

If Mom and Ronnie had ever talked, they might better have seen events from the other's point of view, but in their day and among conservative small-town dwellers like them, folks tended not to talk candidly about anything that really mattered, especially lifelong hurts. No, they were stuck: He felt more vulnerable than ever from the transformation of his face and body, and he couldn't risk being with Mom anyway for fear she'd hurt him all over again, even unintentionally. She did try to connect with him and to help him—she showed up at the barbershop that lipstick-tapping time a few months before he died, and she wrote earnest letters to him as his death approached—but he was too sick and too apprehensive to respond. As for Mom, her guilt concerning Ronnie kept accruing over the years, especially after he went into the hospital. Yet she couldn't bear to share it with even her most compassionate friends, so she never found any relief. He was the shadow over her life, as she was over his, and I wasn't the one to bring them together.

I WAS CAUGHT between these two tall, miserable people all my life. Even before I knew who Ronnie was, I sensed something was deeply wrong with my mother. I saw early on that she was distressed, and it frightened and threatened me in a primal way that defies language. To see your parent suffering is to feel the chill of precariousness, to know that although you might have it good right now, although the lights are burning bright and the family table is bountiful at the moment, it all could fall apart.

ONE OF THE most disheartening realizations about this story came to me late in thinking about it. For years I'd talked with dozens of people who'd known Ronnie—barbershop customers, a girlfriend, landlady Max, and friends stretching from boyhood to the end of his life. Not one of them knew who his mother was. Finally, it dawned on me: Ronnie kept Mom's secret all his life. It had been nearly fifty years since she harshly directed him, "Don't you *ever* call me Mama," and he never did.

REMINDERS OF MOM, Daddy, and Ronnie surround me now at our house on a quiet Roanoke cul-de-sac. I keep my office pens in Daddy's metal cream cup from the milk house. His aluminum milk bucket holds our rolled-up place mats. Hanging in the bedroom is Mom's wide-brimmed straw gardening hat, rigged with an old cloth belt of hers that once tied it around her chin. Each winter our hats and gloves curl up together in Granddaddy Bishop's wooden apple basket. We eat at a round table made from century-old boards Daddy salvaged from a long-demolished Bridlespur barn.

The beam of Ronnie's chrome-plated Eveready flashlight darts around our backyard nightly, signaling for our dog, Sparkle, to come in at bedtime. I trim Dan's beard with Ronnie's barbering shears, and when we eat fontina cheese, we think of the hillbilly boy who peeked over the fence.

EPILOGUE

January 10, 2019

A long-faced older woman in the back row watched with penetrating intensity as I spoke about my book last year at a library outside my Virginia city. After I finished, she walked straight to me and, with tears in her eyes, whispered that, just like my brother, Ronnie, she had been born in 1935 to an unmarried girl. All she said was, "I've had a hard life."

People were lining up for me to sign their books. I hugged the woman but didn't catch her name. I urged her to pick up a bookmark bearing my phone number. I never heard from her.

In years of work on this book, I'd focused on my mother and my brother, and not so much on how they fit into the long history of pregnancies outside marriage. Immediately after the hardback's release, readers began to enlighten me.

I had worried that my mom's oldest surviving female acquaintances, now in their eighties and nineties, would object to me outing her shame over her first pregnancy. But that was not the case. An eighty-eight-year-old with ties to Mom from her rural childhood called to congratulate me on the book.

"But should I have written it?" I asked.

"Oh yes," she replied. "Women had it hard back then, and people need to know."

She and other readers explained to me that a young woman's unwed pregnancy presented an ethical dilemma, not only for her family but for her entire community. The common

reaction was to make an example of her and banish her like a leper so her female friends would observe and know: Get pregnant outside marriage and you'll be very sorry. Never mind who impregnated you, never mind the circumstances. You will always be the one to blame, and in Mom's home of Moneta, Virginia—as in countless other places—forgiveness did not extend to such a girl.

Combine these severe attitudes with the scarcity of services for impoverished, unwed mothers during the Great Depression, and my mom could not have seen much hope for her future. She was fortunate that a church member directed her to a home for unmarried mothers only one county over from Moneta.

As far as I know, Lynchburg's Florence Crittenton Home, one of a chain of homes across the country, only served white women, at least in Mom's racially segregated youth. Her albums from that period contain photo booth shots of young women, almost certainly her dorm mates at Crittenton, and they are all white. How did other groups in the South and elsewhere handle so-called illegitimacies? With a shared history of enslavement, rapes by white masters, disruption of family bonds, and the ripping away of enslaved children and spouses as they were sold and sent away, had African Americans passed more compassion toward mothers down through the generations?

I reached out to black friends to learn how their communities dealt with pregnant girls. One's aunt, born in Virginia not long after Mom, was not banished but given a stern warning not to get pregnant again until marriage. She agreed, and her first child grew up contentedly within the family. Another friend recalled a pregnant girl being forced to stand in her Al-

abama church and apologize to the congregation for her carelessness, even as the soon-to-be father of her child sat beside her in the pew, not called to any account for it.

Just as my mother's sex partner probably never knew he'd upended her early adulthood, the male actors in these frequent dramas were seldom, if ever, disgraced. I heard stories from readers about girls shunned even though they had been impregnated as minors by their own fathers. Down through the ages, it seems to me, women have been punished because our mere physical existence excites the male libido.

I'd hoped that readers would deliver new insights and new information after my book came out, and I wasn't disappointed.

Women readers in particular reacted with deep empathy for my mother. Their most frequent question, not fully addressed in the book, was why Mom refused to allow Ronnie's foster parents, Polly and Roy Hall, to adopt him. If Mom had let him go, Ronnie was unlikely to have lived in a barn, an orphanage, a reform school, or a mental hospital.

From my earliest days, I was well acquainted with the family among whom Mom grew up after her mother's death, when Mom was four. The Hicks family employed her father and provided a cabin for Mom, her dad, and her brother on the grounds of the Hicks home. Each time Mom, Daddy, and I traveled to Moneta to visit my grandfather, we stopped by the homes of Hicks elders. Mom adored them all, though they, like everyone else in her church and elsewhere in Moneta, failed to prevent her removal from the community.

Mom was so stung by Moneta's judgments of her as a bad girl, I believe she wanted more than anything to prove to friends and family back home that she could provide a good

home for Ronnie. Each time she visited the Hickses, they asked her kindly about Ronnie, because to not do so would have seemed impolite. To tell them she had surrendered him permanently by agreeing to his adoption would have humiliated her all over again, or so I think she believed.

The fact that preteen Ronnie slept in barns, then in a self-built mountain cabin, and that he didn't eat with us in his last years on the farm struck some readers as evidence of extreme cruelty on our mother's part. Mom was torn between service to her two children. I was ten years younger, docile, and her husband's biological child, therefore she catered to me, not Ronnie. If Ronnie was acting up and refusing to join us at the supper table, well, she couldn't chase him all over the farm and force him to join us. She didn't handle her responsibilities to him well, and for his part, Ronnie didn't make it easy. He was hurt, angry, and unruly.

Several people shared stories with me about other victims of Ronnie's disorder, acromegaly. I learned about a loving 1940s mother who developed a masculine face and husky voice but didn't let her untreated symptoms get her down. Another, born more recently into a medical family, somehow escaped diagnosis until he enrolled in medical school where a doctor took one look at him and quickly confirmed he had the disorder. His soft-tissue symptoms faded with treatment.

Ralph Berrier, a friend and former colleague at the *Roanoke Times*, ended my puzzlement over why Ronnie's classmates at Miller School came to nickname the skinny boy "Slim Idaho." Ralph, a bluegrass historian and author of *If Trouble Don't Kill Me: A Family's Story of Brotherhood, War, and Bluegrass*, told me that "Slim Idaho" was the stage name of Dewey Hubbard Aderhold Jr., a whiz-bang steel guitar player on forties

radio whose last name sounded vaguely like "Idaho." As it happened, Ralph's granddad and his great-uncle, bluegrass pioneers themselves, had performed with Aderhold on popular Virginia radio shows. Aderhold's accidental death at twenty-three, reportedly while riding his motorcycle to a gig, came during the years Ronnie was at Miller School.

I still haven't identified Ronnie's biological father, long dead. He was quite a bit older than Mom, and she now would be 103. I still hope to figure out which of the many men with his name was the one who lured her with beer to a dark outbuilding that night during the Christmas holidays of 1934.

More than anything, I'd hoped the book would encourage soul-searching within families fractured by secrets like ours. That hope has been borne out as well. People wrote that after reading my book, they were reaching out to estranged siblings. They were rethinking the early lives of troubled parents. They were initiating special one-on-one times with adult children to strengthen those bonds. They were locating surprise siblings, cousins, and children long ago adopted out of their families. In one case, an elderly man just learned that more than fifty years ago, around the time he moved from his hometown, a high school girlfriend had failed to let him know she was pregnant with his child. Shortly after delivering their son, she surrendered him to an adoption agency. That state's adoption records for that period are sealed. The man feels cheated—not only out of participation in his son's life but out of the mere knowledge of his existence.

One of the sweetest surprises the book bestowed on me was the discovery, late in life, that I enjoy giving talks, especially about the book. I'd done very little public speaking before. It's been reassuring to me that in such a divided time in

our nation, strangers will sit together and listen raptly to a sad story about a family as ordinary as mine. In all my talks before hundreds of people, I've caught only one person dozing, and he was sitting in a crowded library room on a cold night, next to a full-blast baseboard heater the staff was unable to shut off.

Through the Keswick grapevine, I heard about a reader who was mildly bothered by the book's unnamed mention of her mother. When I was growing up, Mom often expressed jealousy over Daddy's friendship with Keswick's long-ago female postmaster (as well as with other smart women at church and elsewhere). At the post office, he would lean against the counter as he and the woman jabbered with great seriousness about names, dates, and places boring to me as a little girl. Mom confirmed after Daddy's death that they were just friends. There was an irresistible attraction for Daddy, however. The postmaster, unusually well-read, knew more than most people about my dad's favorite subject: Albemarle County history.

On Halloween Eve 2018, I stood before residents of Keswick and described what it was like to grow up the shy child of servants in such a moneyed place. Grace Episcopal had been where rich residents went to church in my day, and here I was in their parish hall, describing what Keswick was like for people like me.

A remarkable cross-section of people came—my first-grade classmates, estate owners, former household servants, descendants of masters, slaves, and indentured servants. I read passages from the book, about how to this day I sometimes feel a pall of irrational fear drop over me at the voice of a wealthy Southern woman. I talked about Keswick details cut from the

book—such as historical evidence that Keswick landowners, who sent their children to private schools, paid far less in taxes for our public schools than poorer taxpayers elsewhere in the county, leaving my elementary school to make do with outhouses and no running water well into the fifties.

And you know what? The audience embraced what I said. Nobody stormed out. Nobody whacked me with their riding crop. Nobody contradicted anything. They thanked me, hugged me, even kissed me.

They knew that my appearance, as well as my book, was a long-needed truth-telling, with a tender twist. Despite my neurotic fears, I love Keswick just as my parents did. "When I'm on my deathbed," I said in closing that night, "when I'm high on morphine and I take my final breaths, I hope in my mind's eye I'll be seeing the fields of Bridlespur."

ACKNOWLEDGMENTS

THE CUSTOM IS to thank spouses at the end, but in case you don't read all these acknowledgments, I want to say up front that this book could not have happened without Dan Crawford, my husband. He not only vacuumed and shopped and paid bills, he listened, and he understood why I wanted so much to tell this story. Thank you, Dan, for thousands of moments over the years that popped me back onto my path.

My friend Beth Macy brought me soup, introduced me to her agent, educated me on the editing process, and for decades heard my angst over my brother. (Her husband, Tom Landon, encouraged me too, all along the way.) In an initial Beth-urged phone talk with agent Peter McGuigan, he inhaled the heady flavors of my story and quickly shopped around the book proposal he had coached into shape. He and his assistant, Claire Harris, have been guiding the book's progress ever since.

Harper editor Claire Wachtel responded to my proposal first, with intoxicating words of praise. I owe it to her that I found a home at Harper. Editor Sofia Groopman picked it up from there, gently leading me through a total restructuring, hundreds of sensitive edits, and what I thought then were shocking cuts. (You were right, Sofia.)

I've had an extraordinary team at Harper, including publicist Nick Davies, marketing manager Christine Choe, production editor Nikki Baldauf, counsel Victor Hendrickson, interior designer Fritz Metsch, jacket designer Sarah Brody,

and copyeditor Elise Morrongiello, each of whom have been a joy to work with.

No single reader deepened my understanding of my family dynamics more than Charlottesville's Dr. J. Anderson "Andy" Thomson. He knew my parents and the farm I grew up on, and as a bonus, he's a psychiatrist. He helped me see how without Ronnie's initial yearlong attachment to Mom and five years to his foster parents, he likely would have suffered much more emotionally. Andy pointed out how Ronnie's choice to become a barber fed his need for regular, if minimal, closeness. Both Andy and Roanoke psychologist Robert Guthrie helped interpret mental hospital records about the seventeen-year-old Ronnie. Over Ronnie's final months, Drs. Will Truslow, Steve South, and K. LeGree Hallman treated him with great heart. Endocrinologist and acromegaly expert Dr. Mary Lee Vance talked with me more recently about Ronnie's illness.

The people of Virginia's Albemarle County and its environs confirmed memories and offered fresh ones. Thank you, Barclay Rives, brothers Charlie, Harold, and Peter Hallock, Phylissa and Mildred Mitchell, John E. "Jay" Early III, Myrtle White, Lane Goodall, Margia Kidd Kitts, Margaret Brown, Peggy Dudley Byrd, Niya Bates, Joe Collins, Olivia Branch, Jake Carle, Ginny Smith, Bernice Mitchell, Fritz and Claudine Kundrun, Gladys Leake, Blue and Joan Bomar, and Alice Walker Douglas. Lucia "Cinder" Stanton and the Central Virginia History Researchers, especially Edwina St. Rose and Bob Vernon, provided invaluable background. I'm indebted to G. McNeir "Mackey" Tilman, Bill Tilman, and Lynda Daughterty for recollections of Tilman's Department Store. Lorenzo Dickerson's documentaries about Albemarle County's racial history informed my story.

Over the years, many former and current *Roanoke Times* staffers helped with details surrounding my brother's life and lent emotional support, especially Beth Obenshain, Rob Freis, Ralph Berrier, Don Petersen, Lee Wenzler, Chuck Hite, Diane Leach, Tonia Moxley (and Maureen Peters), Mike Hudson, and David Poole. No one helped me believe in my journalism more than my former editor there, Rich Martin. Sue Lindsey, another former newspaper editor, read a later draft and continually bucked me up at critical points.

Other fellow writers and readers buoyed my confidence. Thanks to Christina Nifong, Leigh Anne Kelley, Libba Wolfe, Sandra Kelly, and Laura Scott, as well as Daphne Huffman and Lucy Lee. Alice and Joe Duehl were among the many friends who listened to my story with open hearts, as did Herb Beskar and Cecily Wood, Beth Obenshain and Fred Carlisle, Becky Hepler and Rick Teague, Jim and Cathy Crawford, Mindy Fullilove and Uncas McThenia.

For research on eugenics, which helped put my mother's story in perspective, the Virginia Foundation for the Humanities gave me a fellowship for study, the Fund for Investigative Journalism and the Department of Energy's Office of Science provided funding, and the Virginia Center for the Creative Arts offered a lovely place in which to write. At Hollins University, longtime cheerers-on included Marilyn Moriarty, Ethel Morgan Smith, Jeanne Larsen, Cathy Hankla, and Richard Dillard.

Librarians furnished hundreds of details for this book, especially Edwina Parks, Dyron Knick, and Nathan Flinchum in Roanoke, Carol Glosh in Salem, and, at the *Roanoke Times*, the unstumpable Belinda Harris. Historical societies also: Margaret O'Bryant at Albemarle-Charlottesville, John Long

at Salem, Virginia, and Brenda Baratto at Aiken County, South Carolina. Sherry Lawton-Fasic at Christ Church Christiana Hundred in Delaware confirmed dates for me. Columbus, Ohio, police detective Mike Thomas provided details on my uncle's death there.

For Roanoke history, my go-to resources were (and are) Dr. Reginald Shareef, Brenda Hamilton, Susan Lower, and Paul Garst; for Vinton, it was Nita Echols, Jim Echols, and Dan Smith. Over the phone, David Stewart Wiley's keen ear identified the tune my dad and granddad whistled to their dogs. Over at the house where Mom rented a room in 1936, new owner Danessa Wimmer graciously invited in a stranger to see where her mother stayed most of a century before. Years ago, Francis Willis recalled my sweet young mother when she joined the staff at Hobby Horse Farm, and Alice Trout Hagan drew vivid mental pictures for me of the elder McIntyres. Dorothy Linkous Robinson and Cora Linkous Dickerson filled in particulars about Ronnie's foster family. For information on the Booths, I'm grateful to Susan Scott Anderson and Barrie Booth. Leon C. Johenning II recalled Ronnie's arrival in Lexington, Virginia, as a young barber.

At institutions that harbored young Ronnie, Donnie Wheatley and Carrie McAllister at Boys' Home shared Ronnie's records, and alums Bob Ramsey and Roy Waller remembered details about him; at Miller School, Ronnie's classmates Bill Simms and David Wilson Collier entertained me for hours with their memories.

An informal team kept me healthy as I finished the book: Dr. Clifford Nottingham, nurse practitioner Nancy Harvey, PT Rick Sidor, Dr. Carl Musser, Dr. Vishal Bhagat, Dr. Brian

Gross, and psychotherapists Ron Salzbach, Barbara Horton, and my brethren in our Thursday afternoon group.

Family and near-family were soul mates to me throughout, most of all Buddy and Carolyn McIntyre. Daniel Alan Bishop, Ruth Allison Bane, Shirley Collins, Jean Williamson, Irene and Linda Carter, Bessie Rush Fox, and Kitty Murray Davis shared their stories, as did Dorothy Hicks Palmer, Laura Manning Hicks Morgan, Louise Hicks, Janet Hicks Carter, Glen Hicks, Eleanor Hicks Whorley, Meda Hicks, Watkins Blane, and Kathryn Blane Farmer. Sister-in-law Betty Burke calmed my anxieties with homemade soup and heartfelt listening. Brother-in-law Bob Crawford followed my progress and took my picture. Neighbor Nancy Robison spoiled our cat and dog when I was too busy to.

For those who gave me glimpses of Ronnie's prime years, I'm most grateful to Richard Britt, Ellen Jane Campbell, and the Rev. Clyde Carter, who described for me Ronnie's eccentric friend Will Sloan. Al Hopper spent an afternoon recollecting his travels with Ronnie to golf resorts and other favorite places. For discretion's sake, I'm unable to thank her by her real name, but the woman I refer to as Joyce endured scores of way-too-personal questions to give me a view of Ronnie in his courting days. I'm especially beholden to her.

ABOUT THE AUTHOR

A graduate of Columbia Journalism School, MARY CARTER BISHOP was on the *Philadelphia Inquirer* team that won a Pulitzer Prize for its coverage of nuclear leaks at Three Mile Island. Her *Roanoke Times & World-News* series on poisonings and fraud by exterminators and other pesticide users won a George Polk Award and was a Pulitzer finalist.